How *not* to Murder your Mother

Also by Stephanie Calman

Confessions of a Bad Mother
Confessions of a Failed Grown-Up

STEPHANIE CALMAN

*How not to
Murder your
Mother*

MACMILLAN

First published 2008 by Macmillan
an imprint of Pan Macmillan Ltd
Pan Macmillan, 20 New Wharf Road, London N1 9RR
Basingstoke and Oxford
Associated companies throughout the world
www.panmacmillan.com

ISBN 978-0-230-70740-5

1 3 5 7 9 8 6 4 2

A CIP catalogue record for this book is available from
the British Library.

Typeset by SetSystems Ltd, Saffron Walden, Essex
Printed and bound in the UK by
CPI Mackays, Chatham ME5 8TD

Visit **www.panmacmillan.com** to read more about all our books
and to buy them. You will also find features, author interviews and
news of any author events, and you can sign up for e-newsletters
so that you're always first to hear about our new releases.

To my Mother,

*For the race is not to the swift, nor the
battle to the strong, neither yet bread to the wise, nor yet
riches to men of understanding, nor yet favour to men of
skill; but time and chance happeneth to them all.*

– Ecclesiastes

'Dear God, thank you for the occasional moments of peace and love we experience in this family'. – *Homer Simpson*

Contents

1 ... as Pass Out ...

2 Ober ...

3 Making ...

4 ...

... Lost ...

6 Lost ...

7 Bike Mech ...

... Swiss Cottage ...

9 The Market ...

10 Hitting the Ri ...

Contents

1 As Soon as I Pass Carlisle, I Take a Valium 1

2 One Was Mummy 26

3 Shaking Mixture 33

4 Cul-de-Sac 41

5 Turn Left at Dorchester for the Amazon 50

6 Love Frok Me 60

7 Bride's Mother Revisited 83

8 East of Swiss Cottage and South of Reason 97

9 The Mental Elf 103

10 Hitting the Roof 107

11 Shut Up After the Beep 110

12 Power of Attorney 117

13 Better or Worse? Mum into Granny 124

14 Grow Your Own Memories 131

15 You Don't Know How Lucky You Are 1:
22 Things My Mother Has Never Said 136

16 Getting Out the Knives 143

17 Help Is a Four-letter Word 152

18 I Am Not Becoming Her 1:
Let's Call the Whole Thing Off 164

19 Stairway to Heaven 178

20 Trick or Treat 181

21 I Am Not Becoming Her 2:
Caramba! The Girl Has Hidden the Knob! 191

22 I Am Not Becoming Her 3:
Mission to Explain 198

23 Dear Mrs Bumtrinket 203

24 You Don't Know How Lucky You Are 2:
The Baum Identity 212

25 I Am Not Becoming Her 4: STs in Space 224

26 There's No Such Thing as an –
Ideology–Free Lunch 232

27 Hip, Hip, Oh No 246

28 Don't Make a Special Trip 274

29 I Am Not Becoming Her 5:
The Houmous Pots Are Massing 294

30 How Do You Know I Love You? 308

31 Visiting Ours 318

32 Cry If You Break Your Leg 327

33 Fallen Woman 339

34 Unreadable 351

35 The Second Synagogue 361

Postscript: A Lid on It 365

Acknowledgements 368

1 As Soon as I Pass Carlisle, I Take a Valium

My mother and I are like olive and magenta: each fine in its way, but not on the same sofa. We have *some* things in common. For example, we both make our scrambled eggs without stirring them and we've both dated heroin addicts. But it's not really enough to get us through a weekend. Besides, there is another issue.

I am, in her eyes, a demon control freak with a mania for tidiness and *new things* who unreasonably criticizes the totally normal environment in which she lives.

Of course, it's hereditary. My grandmother drove my mother nuts the same way. And Valerie, my mother's unbelievably tidy younger sister. She only used to go back home to Glasgow once a year. And even then she said, 'As soon as I pass Carlisle, I take a Valium.'

According to Valerie, her first act on arriving at my grandmother's place was to sweep in the front door, straight through the house and into the kitchen, towards the target, my grandmother's 'dreadful' tea towels. These she would pick up and, without breaking her stride, take straight out the back door.

'And then, do you know what I do?' she'd say. 'I don't put them in the bin. No. I don't put them in the bin, because she gets them back out again. No. I go down to the end of the garden and *hurl* them over the fence.'

She always emphasized 'hurl', as if to acknowledge that though there wasn't time to pause on her way to the end of the garden, it was rather a lovely word. And spoken in her Scottish accent, it accumulated several more 'r's, which made it especially pleasurable to listen to as I imagined the tea towels sailing over the fence. Beyond the fence was a wood, into which Valerie rightly assumed my grandmother never went. Yet, somehow, she was convinced that Granny was getting them back, and that on each visit it was the same tea towels she was throwing away. Short of tagging them in some way, as the police do with banknotes, she couldn't prove it. She just *knew*.

About twenty years ago, my mother said to us, 'If

I ever get like that, you will tell me, won't you?' which, roughly translated, means: *If I get to the stage of keeping the same tea towels for thirty-five years, even after they've been thrown into a wood and dragged out again, don't mention it. And especially don't try to buy me any new ones.*

It is my failure to interpret these words correctly that is the cause of tension. That, and other things.

When I was small, she went to parties in fabulous cocktail dresses, with hairpieces and false eyelashes. Now she greets me at the door in a hand-knitted, multicoloured waistcoat, visible in the dark at 200 yards. She has mascara on, but it could have been applied some time ago, perhaps for the first night of *Hair*.

Under the multicoloured waistcoat she's wearing a green silk shirt with a stain on the front. It would be awful enough if she hadn't realized, was losing the plot, but she isn't at all. She is, as she always has been, sharper than me by miles. She not only knows the stain is there. She *wants* it there. Negative energy comes off us both like static.

'Mum . . . you have a stain on your shirt.'

'It's fine.'

It's that bit that gets me.

But I am still trying to get through the door.

Instead of being only partly blocked with the usual large basket containing a single card or letter for posting and box of cardboard for recycling, the hall is now completely full. My husband is getting the bags out of the car, so there are only two of us trying to negotiate our way in – me in forward mode, my mother doing a three-point turn and semi-reversing, but it's enough to cause congestion. The rest of the space is now taken up with some kind of square-based wheeled metal basket, presumably a shopping trolley, though without any canvas it looks like a mobile secure unit for small offenders, perhaps the kids who stole everyone's tools one day at the allotment. Its huge great handle projects right out; come in too quickly – admittedly unlikely – and you'll get a metal bar in your face. I want to shove it out of the way but there's nowhere for it to go. Two minutes I've been here and I'm turning into the sort of person who throws shopping trolleys into canals.

I glance into the sitting room.

The chilly concrete floor, which used to be covered by a perfectly innocent green carpet, is now under something plasticky and almost *shiny*.

'Peter!' I hiss. 'Look at this!'

'Ah, lino . . .' he murmurs, a hint of a nostalgic glow coming into his eyes.

'But it isn't!' I splutter. 'It's some kind of *vinyl*.'

He doesn't seem to be that bothered.

'And look at the pattern!'

That there is a pattern says it all. Some kind of 'texture'; it might have been designed as a screen-saver for people who don't want to be overstimulated. Each time I come, this place is further away from the world I dream of inhabiting, of friendly old furniture a little worn by generations of use, the covers somewhat faded perhaps, but resting on carpet, or big old Persian rugs, and a table we can sit at without our plates actually overlapping. A dreadful image comes to mind of our hard-won sofa being replaced by plastic seats, the last vestiges of good taste disappearing until to spend the day at the old-age drop-in centre will be aesthetically a step up. It feels like some kind of reverse makeover show, or a sinister, *Body Snatchers*-type invasion, where nice, individual furniture is gradually replaced by soulless tat. Where will it end? I go back into the kitchen.

'What's happened to the carpet?'

'I've had it replaced,' she says, not looking me in the eye. It *is* the *Body Snatchers*. She's gone into her dead tone, the one where I expect her next line to be: '*The carpet was trying to escape. It was dealt with.*'

'I can see that. Why?'

'This is better.'

'But it so obviously isn't!'

'It's fine. I'm making the tea, actually, just now.'

'I can't believe you got rid of the carpet.'

The next time we come, the unforgiving surface has been supposedly mitigated by a tiny white sheepskin rug, which lies ineffectually in the middle of the room, like a one-inch toupee on a completely bald man.

Finally we reach the kitchen.

She makes tea and puts a saucer on top of the teapot.

'What happened to the lid?'

I immediately regret this question.

'It's fine. I can't lay my hands on it just now.'

I quite admire her defence of the lid, as if it's not lost or broken but on holiday somewhere. Yet I can't bear its absence, because I feel it will rebound on me.

'Look at her, living it up in her fine house in London while her mother has to use a teapot with no lid.'

'Tch!'

'Can't we get you a new one?'

'No, thank you.'

The teapot she's using is the one she decorated for my father. She painted the name of his house on it, Little Stock Farm, and added some sheep. He didn't personally keep sheep, but rented his field out for grazing, which was how they got into the garden one day and nibbled it to the ground.

This might be a good moment to mention the other teapot, the one I have brought. Every morning she has to go downstairs on stiff knees to make a cup of tea, so my sister and I have bought an electric teapot with which we are rather pleased. Unlike the Goblin Teasmades of the past, it is not sad and stolid, like an early device for treating polio, but round and smart and glass. I hold it out triumphantly.

'What do you think? Pretty good, eh?'

She looks at it suspiciously, as if I have an ulterior motive, which of course I have: it's to save her going up and down the stairs every morning on stiff knees.

'Look – you just plug it in and it makes the tea right by the bed so you don't have to go all the way downstairs!'

'No, thank you!'

'Why don't you want it? It will make your life easier.'

'No, thank you!'

It's a nice, smart object, I absolutely promise you. It can't make her feel 'old'. Anyhow, it's a *teapot*, for God's sake, not a bedpan.

But she never lets me buy her anything for the house. Even a lovely scarf I gave her once – beautiful, not old-ladyish – she thrust back at me as if I had handed her a dead rat. Did she see it as a criticism of her own taste? Is she clinging on to the last few years of her own taste before the Age Police move in and make her have chintz? Well, maybe, but the scarf was five years ago. I tell her I'm leaving the teapot in the bedroom in case she changes her mind.

She makes the tea, filling the kettle with difficulty because its lead is the winner of a competition to find the World's Tightest-fitting Kettle Lead. Never mind hurling tea towels. I want to take that kettle and fire it into space. Next to the tea tin I notice the microwave, a device she's becoming increasingly fond of, though not as the instant-labour-saving appliance it's been marketed as, since there are several jars permanently in front of it, and in case of sudden electrocution or rogue household fires, it's kept unplugged.

'I have some biscuits.'

Not having baked once throughout my entire childhood, she has recently started producing excellent shortbread. We occasionally get some in the post, cocooned in bubble wrap. But today there isn't any, so we resort to the larder, where scores of plastic containers wobble in stacks like a Dr Seuss landscape, housing such culinary essentials as breadcrumbs, broken meringue bits and crumbled chocolate flakes. Biscuits are kept in plastic bags held semi-closed with rubber bands, which is why the Jaffa cakes are hard and the digestives soft.

To reach the shelf I bend down to the small, easy-to-trip-over compost bin with its biodegradable liner bags that smell like dead animals, and the equally dinky pedal bin, lined with carrier bags that don't fit. I throw in a plastic bottle lid I find on the table, but it inevitably goes down the gap between the outside of the bag and the bin. I have said this several times before, so try to make it sound like a new topic.

'Hey, why don't we get you a swing bin? Then the bags would fit and the stuff wouldn't go down the side, and also we wouldn't have to bend.'

Note that I say *we* wouldn't have to bend. This appears to be pretend solidarity on my part to avoid drawing attention to her age – '*We all have stiff knees these days!*' – but in fact I hate bending more than she does. If I had my way, not just my oven but my entire kitchen would be four feet in the air. My other motive is a long-term aim to beat my sister by being the one who gets a new bin into the house first. There is no *official* contest to be first with the bin, just some latent sibling competitiveness on my side.

'This is fine. Just get the biscuits, will you?'

'The thing is, the bags you use are too small, so when you put rubbish in, they just slip off and sink to the bottom and the rubbish all comes out.'

'Yes. They're biodegradable.'

She's deployed two of her favourite tactics here: the fact that the non-fitting bags won't contribute to landfill, and the use of the word 'yes' to mean 'I don't care what you think'. So I'm going to lose the bin war, since in her moral hierarchy, biodegradable beats useful. The bags could be two inches wide or the size of sofa covers; she'd use condoms if they decomposed faster.

Maybe I should clean the bin. I peer over the sink to the windowsill, home to clusters of stiff J-cloths, those green, scrubby things and a recent addition – yellow, flannel-like 'eco' cloths made of a special material that 'doesn't smell', or 'doesn't smell' in the way that people found dead in their homes beside piles of cat food tins don't smell, i.e. not to them. She loves these because you use them without soap or cleaning fluid, whereas I think they're more noteworthy for the fact that they never dry out. Among the clusters a few dusty plants peer out of their pots, possibly wondering why they can't be in the garden with the flourishing vegetation, and also why they are so rarely watered, when they're right next door to the taps.

'Have you got a *clean* cloth?' I ask her, using the Wrong Emphasis.

'Yes,' she says firmly, to mean 'No, but I'm not going to admit it.'

I touch the cloths gingerly, like a child picking up a worm, and a teachery voice in my head says, '*Now, stop being silly.*'

I'm tempted to use her technique of making a point in as roundabout a way as possible: for example, '*Have you thought how useful it would be to have a cleaner?*' But I don't; incredible as it seems, she has one already.

Even more wondrous is the fact that, despite all my mother's attempts to stop her, Mrs W does actually clean. I have seen her doing it. Because my mother is uncomfortable with the idea of employing someone and giving them instructions, which is dangerously close to being a boss, she likes to talk to Mrs W all the time, to show that she is not being superior. And why not? Mum isn't superior and Mrs W is a very nice woman. But it is quite a challenge for her to actually do the job. Leaving aside the layout, the long, thin table bisecting the kitchen, the impossibility of fully opening the dishwasher and that there is nowhere to hang washing or do the ironing, she must also work while being continuously talked at. I witnessed this miracle a few months ago and just had to tell everyone I knew. Not only did she manage to clean the floor, clear the surfaces of clutter and do all the usual stuff, she also wiped up the contents of a tin of varnish which had somehow spilled down the wall in the impossible-to-reach alcove behind the clock – and to lay the table for Lawrence and Lydia's lunch. All while being chatted to, not only by my mother but by me as well, though of course I had a proper reason, which was not trying to bring about the Classless Society, but attempting to discover if any of her other clients were likely to die soon so she'd have more free hours. And the biggest miracle of all? By the next morning there was absolutely no sign that she had ever been there. But in any case my mother doesn't need a cleaner, she needs an archaeologist.

A drink would be a good idea. Or several. I've brought three bottles, which is not just from generosity. The wine rack is under the stairs, in an almost totally inaccessible cupboard, presumably from the Alcoholics Anonymous catalogue. To get into it, I go round the long, thin table that bisects the room, a bit like navigating Cape Horn before the Panama Canal was built, and, being careful not to dislodge the clothes peg under the leg that's too short, crouch right down on the floor and, having moved two chairs out of the way, open the two-foot-high door as conceived by Lewis Carroll and reach in for the wine.

'I'm getting a light for in there actually,' she says, when after all that I emerge without any because the rack is empty except for some ginger wine, some cheap Cava and a bottle of very sweet sherry. There is a light, or more accurately a 'light', attached to the wall with Velcro: a round, stick-on, battery-operated thing that's supposed to come on when pressed, like a giant button. But after about ten goes, the battery ran out. And like all batteries in the universe, it suffers from an inherent weakness, namely its need to be replaced. Somewhere in the house there is a plastic tub full of working – or possibly 'working' – batteries, but she can't lay her hands on it just now. In any case, for all I know she is waiting for a call from the village handyman – whose main attribute is his elusiveness, suggesting that a career in espionage might have suited him better – to tell her when he can come round to change them.

'Mummy,' I say, 'please let us buy you a proper light.'

'This is fine.'

'It doesn't work, though.'

'It's very good, actually. It's from a catalogue.'

Like many of her contemporaries, she is catalogue mad, ordering countless white plastic items that cost little, arrive promptly and break quickly, thus sparing her stressful trips to Canterbury to find a parking space to trail round shops selling lights that actually work. There's a different style of broken lamp in every room, and the ones that do work for some reason have no shades. They sit forlornly on the edges of wobbly tables, their naked low-energy bulbs emitting a sad white light, like the smiles of African orphans hoping to be adopted.

So I bring my own wine. I pour some for us, then realize that in order to keep it cold, I'm going to have to Open the Fridge.

You *can* open the fridge, but not if the table has been moved out by more than an inch, and not if anyone is loading the dishwasher. Try to chill the wine *and* get a clean glass, and you have gridlock.

I bend down and look in. On the top shelf is the yoghurt colony. When she buys a new one, she pushes it in until the out-of-date ones are at the back. The middle shelf is home to two half-eaten packets of rancid butter, with knife gouges like evidence of an attack by lapsed vegans, a fresh chicken covered with a bowl and a margarine tub with about three molecules of margarine in it. There are also the ends of two leeks in a brown paper bag, some mushrooms like a very old person's testicles and half a red pepper looking like a botched episiotomy. And at the bottom there is a huge bowl of chicken stock that, when I try to move it, spills on my shoes.

The door, where the wine will have to go, is full of chutneys and jars of curry sauces. Very quietly, with my back to her, I take out the chutneys and curry sauces and move my wine into the space. There is also a jar of black olives, its liquid intriguingly depleted. Has it simply evaporated over time, or has she been drinking it? Next to that is a jar of pickled walnuts which I'm sure I recognize; I think it came with her from the previous house.

'I've got a farmers' market chicken.'

'Oh, lovely!'

'Peter, would you mind getting the potatoes?'

'Sure. Where are they?'

'In the downstairs loo.'

He gives me a *'don't say anything'* look and vanishes into the recently installed freezing lavatory. It has a 'heater' – a kind of decorative cylinder under the sink – and two bins: a tiny chrome pedal bin whose lid jams the moment you put anything in it, and a small, traditional-style steel bin, which contains the potatoes.

What I should do now is take my drink and go into the other room, or upstairs or outside to sweep the path, or anywhere, and not watch her Trying to Open the Oven. But I don't.

She *can* open it, but only by getting a chair from the collection of chairs – some of which can be sat on but you never know which ones – that congregate in the kitchen and sitting room. I've tried on previous visits to remove one or two in a surreptitious, musical-chairs kind of way, so we can get round the room more easily, but am not allowed. She needs them all in case she suddenly has to invite ten people round – which, to be fair, she sometimes does, to her archive group, although I think when they all come they have to sit in two separate rooms while she dashes back and forth like a surgeon with a very full list.

She puts the chair in front of the oven door, which is unbelievably hard to open, not because her hands are getting stiff but because it's been design-ed to withstand extreme force, such as I don't know what: break-ins by people bent on stealing half-cooked chickens. Even I have to pull like mad, although it's academic because she won't let me. I watch her trying to move the oven shelves, which hook into narrow, curved slots so if you want to move them around they have to be lifted and pulled at exactly the right angle, like disabling the nuclear device at the end of a James Bond film. Get it wrong and there's the sound of metal grating against gravelly oven wall, like crashing gears. I want to know what kind of person builds an oven that you have to fight your way into. Maybe it's from a line designed for combat duty; the others in the range were an Apache gunship wine cooler and a Chieftain tank biscuit tin.

'Can I do it?'

'No.'

She gets down slowly from the chair and struggles to manoeuvre it back round the other side of the table, not because she's feeble but because the room is so full.

'Shall I lay the table?'

'That'd be nice, yes.'

In order to do this I have to move the money-off vouchers, used envelopes, dried-up felt pens, the TV listings from the local paper, parish magazine, Lakeland catalogue, packet of seeds, half-completed shopping list, letter from a local campaign group about the community farm proposal, and several inserts from the Sunday papers advertising walk-in baths, elasticated trousers or other hideous accessories of old age for which she is not yet – I hope to God – ready.

Or rather, I want to move them. She likes to keep the pile there while we eat. But the table is already impossible for more than two people to eat on, being precisely twenty-two inches wide. So everyone's plates touch. And forget having anything else on there, like food. So while she's struggling with the oven door I grab the whole pile and sneak it out into the hall. I also drag out the red plastic box full of magazines for recycling that lives under there, taking up the tiny amount of space available to put your feet.

The cutlery's in the cutlery drawer, but a lot of the china is stacked in piles in the floor-level cupboards. These patterns date back as far as her last boyfriend, who favoured eating off rough-hewn dishes made of wood as if from a pantomime of *Goldilocks*, and a period when a friend of hers got divorced and opened a china shop, and would come round with various bargains and special offers. None was to her taste, but as she couldn't say no for fear of offending, she still lives with several gold and white tea sets. The rest of the plates, including my favourite willow pattern ones, are on the shelves, though only just. The shelves are suitable for anything except plates, since there are big gaps at the back through which plates can easily fall. This is because they've been fixed on with the brackets upside down, holding them like arms carrying trays, as opposed to underneath. So the shelves stand away from the wall, allowing anything narrower than an eggcup to slip through. And so I say what I can't stop myself from saying, what I said the last time I was here.

'Why on earth did he leave those bloody great big gaps?!'

And she says, 'His marriage was breaking up.'

Pretty much every job she's ever had done in this place has been carried out by men with some kind of aesthetic disability or emotional problem that rendered them unable to butt pieces of wood against walls. The only normal one fitted the cooker, and that has insurgent-proof doors. Actually it isn't just this house. In the flat where I grew up nothing was fitted sanely either, but that was due to morning sickness.

'I couldn't issue instructions to workmen; I couldn't even get up.'

This apparently explains why we had a coal store with no opening to get the coal out, a record player you could only plug in by lying on the ground and reaching under a shelf two inches off the floor, and an abnormally thin 'breakfast counter' designed as if for a caravan, which allowed people to squeeze past on their way to do the washing-up, but wasn't wide enough for you to eat at without your nose touching the wall. And we all have quite neat noses.

I got out of the car a forty-year-old mother and career person; now I'm leaning sullenly against the doorway, my lower lip stuck out, waiting for my sixteenth birthday to hurry up so I can threaten to move out. As I stepped over the threshold, the years slipped away. Feel younger fast! No pills, creams or surgery! Just visit your mother and go back to your adolescence.

I'm feeling like a teenager, but with the burdens of a parent. Of course I feel responsible: I bloody *am*. Her top has a stain on it. Have the neighbours seen?

'At least let me buy you a new shirt,' I plead.

'It's fine. I only use it for travelling.'

'You mean you went on the *train* like that?'

'It's fine.'

So this is how she used to feel if I ever tried to leave for school with a hole in my tights. I don't want her to go around in a stained shirt because it makes *me* look bad.

A few years back, Peter had an idea he thought would help reduce the 'potential for conflict' between me and my mother. His sister Jessica had a dog called Rosie, who went bananas when anyone came to the house, or at least when I did, since dogs, as we know, always identify the least dog-tolerant person in the room and devote all their attention to them for the duration of their stay.

I don't 'hate dogs', by the way. I just object to eating dinner while one gnaws a bone the size of a human femur right next to my feet. Rosie also made a habit of charging without warning from one end of the room to the other, as if she had seen a dead pheasant, or whatever her ancestors had been bred to fetch, and had to bring it back RIGHT NOW. Peter sat through these meals embarrassed by my involuntary shudderings and causing marital tension by never once asking her to take Rosie out, so that by the end of the meal there were always two sources of growling. I was amazed, therefore, when Jessica announced she was seeing a trainer.

The trainer was teaching her to follow a simple series of reward-induced activities apparently guaranteed to alter her behaviour. She was then encouraged to apply these to the dog. The training centred round a metal tray, to be banged sharply when it disobeyed instructions or played up too much.

It was too much for Peter to resist.

'Hey, we can do that at your mother's!' he said as we packed our stuff into the car.

'I'm sorry?'

'Well, I probably won't bang an *actual tray . . .*'

'Good, because that would stop the argument by giving her a stroke.'

'But if you two – "start", I'll just bark the word "tray" in your ear.'

That particular weekend we turned up, and all fears of a disagreement melted away when she asked me to help tidy out her wardrobe. My mother, asking me to Help Her Tidy. This was like the Americans asking for a bit of a hand with their foreign policy.

'I would absolutely *love* to,' I said, having to be held back by Peter from actually tearing off the wardrobe door.

'I'm aware that it has become rather – *full*,' she conceded. It was *so* full that she'd named it the 'Augean Cupboard', after the Fifth Labour of Hercules – I had to look it up – in which he had to muck out the Augean Stables, home to hordes of – presumably endlessly pooing – cattle.

So we made tea and went upstairs and opened the cupboard and the stuff just came bursting out. Duvets, spare curtains, unfeasible numbers of brightly coloured silk shirts: they came, and kept on coming, like an alien autopsy.

There was a pair of jeans belonging to my sister's last boyfriend but one; the sheets alone told the history of British textile design over the last thirty years. When we found several shirts belonging to Mum's boyfriend Graham from the late 1970s – and his purple, blue and brown, hexagonal, fake-patchwork duvet cover – we realized that from this one cupboard a whole side of the family could be carbon-dated. If you chopped a section down the middle of the mound now filling the bedroom, it would look like the excavation of Troy, though King Priam was probably a stranger to drip-dry.

We pulled and piled, and pulled and piled. We pulled out the drawer under the bed to store the things she *was* keeping, only to find it contained six anoraks. And still it went on. We were drowning in duvets and jumpers, and the cupboard was still not empty. More unfamiliar sets of curtains spilled out in sedative pastels, and we could only conclude the thing was backless, as in *The Lion, the Witch and the Wardrobe*, and that this was the entire linen supply of the house next door.

Not surprisingly, my mother was soon ready for a lie-down. The sheer sight of that much garishly patterned sheeting had taken its toll and she staggered weakly to her room. We persuaded her to part with about half the mound, chiefly the lurid, ex-boyfriends' shirts and faux-patchwork bedcovers, but she balked at being separated from the rest. Luckily, the cupboard was in the spare room, so we decided to smuggle the rest – the moth-eaten mohair sweaters, faux-patchwork pillowcases and anoraks – out of the house while she slept.

However, the stairs were very narrow, and the garden – in keeping with the general 'look', as they say in magazines – was littered with pots on top of each other, which toppled and wobbled and crowded on to the path, making progress to the gate somewhat challenging.

'I know,' said Peter. 'I'll bring the car round the side and we can push the stuff out of the window.'

I liked this idea. It reminded me of when my sister and I were moving my old desk from the bedroom to the sitting room and it fell apart, right there in the doorway. We carried it out in armfuls to a skip.

So Peter brought the car round and I posted a stream of weirdly coloured shirts and bedlinen out of the window for him to catch, to the wonderment of the people sitting outside the tea room opposite.

He made three trips to the dump. The job was done and euphoria descended. My mother had the look on her face of someone who has just had a lump removed. We gathered in the kitchen for tea. Just then, a sauce bottle leapt from a shelf, unable to bear the overcrowding, and smashed my grand-mother's glass salt dish on the counter beneath.

'Bloody hell, Mother!' I snapped.

'*Tray!*' barked Peter.

And she looked up.

'Mm, dear? Très what?'

If only all our visits could be as relaxing as this.

2 One Was Mummy

About two years after my parents separated, my mother joined a club for divorcees. To be exact, the leaflet said 'For divorced, separated, widowed and single people', but they were almost all divorced.

A discrepancy in the calibre of the two sexes quickly emerged. After a few evenings she told us, 'The women talk to each other and the men carp about their ex-wives.'

But even if she feared she might not find Mr Almost Right there, Mum made her mark by designing the programmes, which featured elaborate comic-strip panels of lecherous men flinging obscurely obscene puns at coyly flattered women. The one about swimming – 'Not THAT breast-stroke!' – always sticks in my mind, although one should remember that this was 1968; men did not wear deodorant, women were still chicks and dolly-birds, and wives did not automatically get half of anything in a divorce.

The members took turns to host the parties and when it was Mum's turn, my sister and I would creep out of bed to monitor proceedings from behind our bedroom door. We were big Miss World fans at the time and gave everything marks out of ten: make-up, clothes and especially accents. Shawls and ponchos were big then, the kind worn by well-read people who haven't shopped in a while. We soon started to look out for regulars whom we moulded into characters with catchphrases or hilarious mannerisms. There was a woman called Joy who played the guitar; we impersonated her performing household tasks like washing up while constantly strumming. A psychiatric nurse in a leather waistcoat called Helmut announced one night he had brought 'Ze zendvich matehials', i.e. bread and cold meat, and thenceforth Zendvich Matehials became his name. At seven Claire was already a confident mimic and Mum always laughed at our post-party reprises the next day. So appreciative was she, in fact, that we only had to say, 'Zendvich Matehials!' in the middle of dinner, or better still while she was on the phone, to make her crack up.

We made up a rhyme about them, based on a surreal counting book, *One Was Johnny*, by Maurice Sendak – author of *Where the Wild Things Are* – which began: 'One was Johnny, who lived by himself; Two was a Rat who jumped on the shelf; Three was a Cat who jumped on the Rat; Four was a Dog who came in and Sat.' And so on, up to ten.

This became: 'One was Mummy, who lived by herself; Two was Sal, who jumped on the shelf; Three was Osbert, who jumped on Sal!'

Sally was a close friend of our mother's and Osbert a local book dealer who, legend had it, had lived for twelve years on bread and Marmite. He never to our knowledge made any moves on Sally, but we liked the way it sounded. 'Four was Wilf, who came in and sat,' we added, jumping up and down with excitement. This was, we thought, extremely apt, as Wilf looked like doing just that.

Wilf didn't have a catchphrase. Among the red-faced men, and women in beads and velvet hats, he stood out in his braces and stripy, drip-dry shirts. He spoke with a Yorkshire accent – Hull – and put Brylcreem on his hair. He wore deodorant. He was intelligent but without intellectual pretension, and unlike the others didn't complain about his ex-wife – for two reasons: one, she wasn't his ex-wife yet, and two, he wasn't the carping type. They still technically lived at the same address with their five children, although her boyfriend had by then moved in. Even though Wilf was a GP and she a teacher, this was all conducted as if it were completely normal. My father had by now moved back into our building with our stepmother, so clearly Wilf was the ideal man to succeed him.

We loved him. He was incapable of being fake or patronizing and his casual affability was a welcome contrast to Dad's volatility. He took us on holiday to his cottage in Ireland, and Mum brought him on our annual trip to Glasgow to introduce him to her parents. He was from the suburbs, a place my mother had no time for. His relationship with the countryside, with which she felt such a deep connection, consisted of getting in the car and going for a drive in it, provoking in her a kind of awestruck comic horror. Yet she indulged him. They found a house in Wiltshire, near a practice he was going to join, and we packed up to move.

The Unhealthy Doctor is a tired old joke, but unfortunately Wilf was it. He smoked heavily and ate fried bread or toast with thick slices of butter, sometimes sprinkled with salt. He took no exercise, as I say, and rarely got out of the car. Before the end of our first summer in the new house, he died suddenly of a stroke. He was forty-six, the age I am now.

As he was still married and had made no will, my

mother had to sell the house they hadn't even begun to pay for and move back to London. Her only mementoes were one photograph, his blood pressure kit and a set of brown glass cups and plates he gave her one Christmas, which at thirty-five years old now qualifies as retro.

In the period that followed she dated Clive, a polite, rather monosyllabic man who waited silently for her in the hall, as if by coming in further he might be tainted by domesticity, and Bill, who was much jollier and came full of smiles and loaded with Mars Bars and Quality Street. Sadly, he was married. He was succeeded by Stan, an ex-colonial, who installed himself at the head of the table as if we'd been waiting for him, and reminisced about his youth as a manager in '*Keenya*'.

'I've worked with Africans,' he said. 'They've got nothing but bone between their ears.'

Mum was entirely without prejudice, so it was all the more shocking to hear this go unchallenged. He also told us men were more intelligent than women, another view we had never heard expressed in our own home. When I said, 'That's not true actually,' he raised his newspaper and, in the middle of the meal, began to read it.

She kept saying how kind he was after her

bereavement, so when he asked her to marry him, we were terrified she might say yes. She finally ditched him when he announced he didn't like Woody Allen. Looks were exchanged across the table and we knew that was it.

After Stan came Graham. He lived in Kent, near the cottage, and despite my father's misgivings – he was clearly no Wilf – Mum invited him to move in. His weird behaviour showed up almost immediately, with long silences during which he would not reply to anything. Mum would say, 'He has hysterical aphonia' – in other words, deafness caused by some emotional problem, rather than being a selfish pain in the arse. Claire and I knew it would end badly, but all we could do was wait.

While Mum was with us during the week in London, Graham had the place to himself. He paid no rent, bought no shopping and used her Mini without once putting in any petrol. Then she discovered that the money from the pictures he was selling for her was staying in his pocket as well. Things got more and more difficult, and eventually she asked him to move out. When she came down the following Friday, she found some of her things, including her hairdryer, in the incinerator in the garden, half burned. He had gone, but some time later came back, and she refused to let him in. He broke the front door open and she ran up to the bathroom, locked the door and called to a neighbour. The police came and, there not having been an assault, he was Bound Over to Keep the Peace. He reportedly moved back to his mother's, but for years Mum wouldn't even go to the same town, just in case. Even after he died she wouldn't go.

Graham was the last. She once asked us, when we were still quite young, who we would most like her to live with. And we said Peter, who had two counts against him. First, he was gay, and second, he was planning to become a woman. Mum, and indeed Peter himself, explained it all to us, and she took us to see him in hospital after the operation, where he greeted us in characteristically breezy mood. Then he moved away to his new life as Petra, and One was Mummy once more.

3 Shaking Mixture

When, just occasionally, I mention to another parent my nine-year-old daughter's fondness for flouncing out of the room during an argument, growling, 'SORR-*EEE*!' they'll often say, 'Ha, just you wait till she's a teenager!'

And I think: *She can never be worse than I was.*

At eleven I was good at maths, keen on Latin and head girl of my primary school. By thirteen, I'd discovered boys.

The tsunami of hormones combined with my low opinion of myself to reduce my interest in fractions and declensions to a pale backdrop behind the all-consuming quest for a boyfriend. In my diary I wrote, 'Haniff crossed the road specially to talk to me!' about the boy at the drama club who provided my first snog. I started spending weekends at my friend Tilly's house, partly to get away from my father and stepmother, and because Tilly's mother took us to Brick Lane market, where we were allowed to eat sweets for breakfast and browse for 1950s clothes. I started a flirtation with one of the stallholders, who gave me free make-up.

My mother's reaction to this change of priorities was unusual.

She had a better understanding than anyone I've ever met of the need of girls to be admired. Though the most glamorous mother by miles, she was without vanity. She assembled the tools of her beautification methodically, as if lining up the ingredients for a recipe. She went out for the evening in hairpieces or 'falls', as women did then, and false eyelashes, which we would find in the morning lurking like spiders by the bathroom mirror. When she came in after a date and kissed us, the scent of sophistication, with hints of cigarette smoke, wine and perfume, wafted round us. We called it the Evening Smell.

Recently I had my first experience of an attractive man looking straight past me to Lydia, and realized how lucky I was that my mother never tried to compete with me. Mind you, as a teenager I wasn't exactly a threat. When I filled out it wasn't just in two places, my skin became greasy overnight and there was the ever-present issue of my body hair.

From the moment dark down first appeared on my upper lip in the last year of primary school, my mother – a fellow sufferer – was out scouring the chemists' shelves for something to bleach it. Superfluous facial hair not being top priority for the pharmaceutical industry, she was dismayed to find that I had to use the same stuff as she had forty years before. Once applied, hydrogen peroxide fizzed dramatically with ammonia fumes that went straight up our noses, so we stood in front of the mirror with our mouths distended like Kenneth Williams pantomiming shock in a Carry On film. For a while we tried something from Hungary labelled 'Shaking Mixture' that was only marginally less pungent. When Jolen Creme eventually arrived in the shops from America, it was like the appearance of the first oranges after the war. The three of us, mother and two daughters, lined up to try the wonderful new product. It fell off in lumps as it dried, bleaching bits of the carpet. But it worked, the flat smelled less like a chemical works and I was able to have a social life.

Meanwhile, other mothers at my clever school tried to combat the blight of adolescence in their daughters with lectures and threats of – horrors – a life without Oxbridge. It's another thing I've only realized since becoming a mother myself: how rare is the middle-class parent who *doesn't* base a sizeable element of their own self-esteem on their children's exam results. Despite her powerful intellect, my mother had no truck with those whose love is conditional on As. It was she, not we, who complained about the amount of homework we got.

'I just think it's too much,' she'd say, shaking her head. And she was bemused by the behaviour of the tense, over-educated women who hogged all the time at parents' evenings.

'Of course I love to hear good things about *you*,' she'd laugh. 'But hopping from foot to foot behind those women going on about whether Persephone is top in maths, Greek *and* cello – my God!'

The school made up for it in ways of which she did approve: no uniform, no discernible rules and therefore no good or bad conduct marks, and alongside the emphasis on Oxbridge, a leaning towards groovy self-expression. She thought it perfectly natural that grammar-school girls should spend their lunchtimes dancing to Elvis records, organizing beauty contests and, in the summer terms, sunbathing. When the big Biba store opened in Kensington, a glorious cathedral of hitherto unimagined make-up colours, I wasted no time in getting down there to try them all, coming home – aged fourteen – liberally doused in an eyeshadow called Midnight. This too was fine.

Occasionally, a line was drawn – literally, one night, with chalk along the sitting-room carpet, when I came home at 12.45 after a disco and confessed to having drunk three halves of lager with a Greek Teddy boy called Phil. And we had a pretty heated encounter over my attempt at the Gypsy Look, which briefly swept the nation in about 1976. She caught me at the front door at 8 a.m. in an off-the-shoulder blouse and white Victorian petticoat and sent me back to change. It was the only time I can ever remember her criticizing my choice of clothes; when I stand arguing with Lydia, who wants to go everywhere – including weddings – in ripped jeans and oversized T-shirt, I realize I got off incredibly lightly.

She also understood the importance of privacy. Right from when I wrote 'Privet' on my bedside drawer when I was six, she kept out of our stuff. She never tidied our rooms – tidying not in any case being one of her passions – and so by extension did not 'accidentally' discover secret diaries or the phone numbers of boys. At fourteen I announced I could no longer share with my sister, then eleven, who annoyed me not just by being alive, but because she was now regularly committing the heinous crime of sitting under her desk reading a comic while boyfriend Dave and I sat staring dismally into space.

'It's my room too,' she repeated, in her most infuriating little-sister tone.

My mother refused to evict her, but eventually – there being only two bedrooms in the flat – gave me the sitting room.

'It'll be like three bedsits!' she said.

And sure enough, our relationship took on a more flatmate-ish quality. Friends who came for dinner, whether ours or hers, were crammed round the table in the strangely shaped kitchen, the result of a conversion in which most of the middle had been scooped out to make the bathroom. To watch TV we gathered in her room and sat on her bed. The summer Billie Jean King beat Evonne Goolagong at Wimbledon, we came home from school each day to watch the tennis together, the telly on the art storage units, our afternoon tea of Hovis and smoked mackerel on our laps. It was the closest I ever got to being a student.

School continued to recede in importance for me except as a place to see my friends. I was desperate for independence and ready cash, and in the holidays before the sixth form temped as a secretary in various dull offices. But instead of getting an early warning of the grim future which awaits the unqualified female, I let the wages – so much greater than mere pocket money – go to my head. School was just too *immature* for me, I decided. Anyway, I couldn't *stand* any more exams, so I wasn't going to go back. I'd been offered a trial as a secretary in a PR firm and really thought I was a grown-up. I announced that nothing would hold me back.

'Well,' she said, 'there are some really good books on the English list. Why don't you stay on and read them? You don't have to take the A level if you don't want.'

She felt more passionately about the only other subject I had managed to keep up, French. After a series of clashes with my teacher, I announced I was giving it up. Having lived in Nantes after the war, where she designed window displays for a department store and adored everything French – including her boss – Mum was, finally, pushed beyond endurance. It was the one time she got my father to come over and bully me into submission.

I did go back, *and* suffered French Lit with Racine and his deadly seventeenth-century rhyming couplets. But with encouragement from my father, I also started my career. When I admitted to bunking off one afternoon to record my first radio piece, my mother recognized a kindred spirit. She had horrified her bluestocking teachers by becoming a *commer-*

cial artist and regarded a creative vocation as sacrosanct. Besides, she had worked on magazines most of her life and never viewed them as second best to 'literature' or anything else.

Again, it was something I took for granted. Recently I was moaning about some awful remark she'd made to me on the phone and my friend Stephen, who was stuck listening while I made dinner, said, 'You're just so lucky. I always wanted to be a journalist and in my family it just wasn't an acceptable choice. I had to become a banker instead.'

The lesson, I guess, is that in order to be happy, you must live the life that's right for you. Everything else leads to misery. No doubt Lydia will soon be reminding me of this in a few years, when I try to talk her into an uncertain future as an artist only to find her secretly studying the derivatives market so she can rebel by becoming a hedge fund manager.

4 Cul-de-Sac

It is the 1980s and my mother has moved full-time to the country to get away from the teeming, vicious metropolis. I arrive at the station to see her waving at me from her usual spot by the timetables. But when we get to her village, she doesn't turn into the lane that leads to the cottage, parking instead on the main road.

'What are you doing?' I say. I can already sense that this is a symptom of a Bigger Problem.

'It's fine.'

I get a tight feeling in my stomach, 'It's fine' being her response to anything bad, or rather, anything bad she doesn't want me to do anything about.

'Why are you parking here?'

'I'll explain later. It's fine.'

'No, I want to know now.'

'I'm not parking in the lane any more.'

'Why not?'

'It's fine.'

'It's not fine. Why can't you park there as normal?'

'Brian and Janice have two cars now. They can't spare the space.'

'But we've been parking there for – whatever, twenty years. Way before they moved in.'

'Yes, but strictly speaking they were doing it as a favour. That bit of the lane actually belongs to them.'

'Well, yes, they were doing it as a favour, in the same way they were being human beings as a favour. So as not to be arseholes.'

'No, no. You don't understand.'

'So now you have to walk all the way down there in the rain. What's to understand?'

'We've agreed that I'll park on the main road.'

'You mean you've agreed to let them bully you.'

'No, no. It's nothing like that.'

I am furious: furious that this is happening to her, and furious that she's pretending it's some kind of choice. Couldn't she at least call it by what it is? But she refuses to talk about it any more and when I leave, we go up the lane to the car tensely, both hoping we won't bump into them. She doesn't want to bump into them because she's afraid I'll yell at them, like my father used to do, and I don't want to bump into them because I don't want to witness her being even more submissive than usual. Despite what she says, I'm not 'just like my father'. When I'm this angry, I stare at the ground.

On my next visit, she mentions casually that she is going to chop a chunk out of her modestly sized garden to make a parking space.

'Whooah! Hang on! Why?'

'It's what we've agreed.'

'Who's agreed? It'll ruin the garden.'

'I don't have the right to park in the lane and parking at the top isn't satisfactory.'

'But a great big bit out of the garden . . . This is – ridiculous.'

I don't, of course, have the solution to this problem. So I keep saying how ridiculous it is in the hope that I will think of one. When my parents bought this place, in 1964, no one had more than one car except the Queen. More to the point, the neighbours weren't so awful. Well, they were, but in a different way. They complained about my sister and me playing noisily in the garden while their small, charmless dogs yapped all day. One even bit me on the leg. But this lot! They wouldn't have dared push my mother around like this when my father was there. In those days, if there was any bullying to be done, it would have been done by him.

She rummages in the cupboard and takes something out of a small plastic container and swallows it.

'What's that?'

'It's nothing. A Valium.'

'What the hell are you taking Valium for?'

'It's been quite stressful, if you want to know.'

'Of course I want to know. You can't just let them – do this!'

I want to go round and punch him, this *Brian*, with his horrible stick-on porch and dull, colourless children, and because she won't even let me talk to him, I've gone from being angry with him to being angry with her.

I want to say to him, '*Oh, so this is what you do, is it, push old women around?*'

But my mother isn't actually old yet, more the upper end of middle-aged, so it's more: '*Is this what you do, then, push slightly older women around?*'

She changes the subject by taking me round the garden. She's done it beautifully, reshaping the traditional layout with its narrow path up the side into something more curvy. It looks twice as big as it used to, and the pergola put in by her transsexual friend Peter – now called Petra – is covered with clematis. But I am fuming.

She is saying something about the hedge. On the

side of the garden that borders the narrowest bit of the lane, the bit you walk down after you've parked your car up on the wide bit – the bit that's *easily wide enough for two cars for most of its length*, it's her hedge on one side and the Batleys', the people opposite's, on the other, forming a sort of channel. My sister and I loved this bit when we were kids. Too small to see over the top, we'd break into a run, anticipating the moment where the hedges ended and we saw the cottage, covered in white roses.

The Batleys, whose hedge formed the other side of the tunnel, had a much lower hedge than ours. Theirs you could see over, even we children could, on to the neat lawn with its tulip and rose borders.

One Friday, we unpacked the car and came down the narrow bit, and my father stopped suddenly.

'What is it?'

After four or five years of marriage, my mother had grown used to sudden changes of mood on his part, though that never stopped her from performing her trademark gasp, often accompanied by clutching whatever piece of furniture came to hand. In the lane, she had to clutch at the hedge. Only it wasn't where she expected it to be.

'He's cut the fucking hedge!'

'What? Oh, no. I'm sure he hasn't. Who?'

'Fucking Batley! Fucking arsehole! He has! Look!'

And sure enough, the top and side, usually round and of varying lengths, were squared off.

'Right . . .'

'Oh no! Please don't say anything!'

Somehow she must have persuaded him not to go round there and scream abuse at him, my father's usual style of conflict resolution. What did happen, though, is that Batley did it again. And my father did go round there and did accuse him, and Batley said he was perfectly within his rights, because our hedge was untidy and didn't fit in. And what happened after that was not that my father thumped him, as my mother feared, or that it escalated into one of those neighbour disputes you read about that start with a leaning fence and end up with someone blasted to bits with a shotgun. Instead, my father came back to the cottage and decided that Mr Batley was a Nazi.

This wasn't *entirely* an irrational leap of his twisted imagination, since Batley clearly had the sort of love of extreme uniformity that in Dad's mind allied him with totalitarian regimes. In his mind, it was square hedges today, rows of goose-stepping storm troopers tomorrow. Clearly, anyone capable of cutting some-one else's hedge to make it the same height as their own was equally capable of getting everyone in the village to stand in a line with one arm in the air. Just think, when in a newsreel about the Third Reich do you ever see a straggly hedge, an unkempt garden – or even a slightly uneven verge?

'You know he would,' he was saying to my mother, when we came in from the swings for supper.

'Would what? Who?'

'Hand over us Jews.'

By now my father had gone from neat hedges to mass deportations, pausing only to fork in large mouthfuls of fish and chips.

Technically, we weren't even properly Jewish, as my mother isn't, but Dad more than made up for that, not by observant practices – he followed none of the rules on diet or anything else – but with his vehemence. Most of the time he wasn't particularly Jewish at all, but the minute he got in the company of someone in whom he detected even the tiniest whiff of anti-Semitism, or anti-Semitic *potential*, he became belligerently, deliberately Jewish.

Sometimes, he was right. During a row that erupted at work one day, his art director said, 'Oh, shut up. If it wasn't for us, you lot would have all ended up as lampshades.'

Faced with that, who *wouldn't* become more Jewish?

Eventually, Dad escaped Überführer Batley by divorcing my mother and buying a second cottage with my stepmother five miles away. The new one had no neighbours at all.

Then one day my mother was kneeling behind her hedge weeding when she heard the Batleys yelling at each other in their garden.

'Go to your fancy woman!' yelled Mrs Batley at full volume. 'Go on then!'

Not so neat after all, eh?

I'm thinking about this as I listen to my mother talking about someone having cut the hedge *again*. Only this time it's colourless Brian.

'He said the lower branches were sticking out and making his children's feet wet.'

'*What*? You are joking.'

'I know: it's silly.'

'Well, just ignore it and tell him to piss off.'

'Oh, there's no point talking to you. Anyway, his lawyer—'

'His *what*?!!'

'They got a lawyer to measure the width of the lane and apparently my hedge is two inches too wide or something. They have the right to do that, you know.'

'Yeah, they have the *right* to behave like complete

shits. It's just that most people choose not to. At least let me go round and stick up for you. This is – insane.'

'No. Thank you.'

'So you're just going to let them carry on?'

'You don't understand living in a community.'

If she means that in my cut-throat urban world of Tarmac, tube trains and skinny mocha lattes I can't possibly appreciate the cosy values of a place where your neighbours bully you so effectively you end up on tranquillizers, she's right: I can't.

5 Turn Left at Dorchester for the Amazon

'The whole of Kent is going to be built on,' my mother declares one day. 'I must move.'

This isn't as crazy as it sounds. The field behind her cottage has been earmarked for housing and already signs are going up heralding the imminent creation of estates with names like The Groves and Green Meadows. The field with the pond where we used to look at the bulrushes has already been covered with 'executive homes'.

'How can it be Green Meadows when they're paving over the fucking meadows to build it?!' she sputters.

She is a fierce defender of green spaces and has succeeded in uniting New Agers and ex-army officers against the coming development, so far to no avail. Also inspired by her, they have tried – and sadly failed – to prevent the building of a football stadium with huge floodlights nowhere near the town it is supposedly serving but in a field right outside the village. She has organized a survey for the local branch of the Green Party, asking people in nearby Ashford, 'What do you want from your environment?' and when the answer 'Something to do' came, she duly listened and sent it on. Her one victory, the preservation of a verge by the A20 containing rare wild flowers, is not adequate consolation. When I pass the verge, the sight of the tiny notice banning the council from strimming it gives me a little thrill of pride. But I see her point. She has to live there. I'm in London, where if I want to breathe I can go to the park. She's in Kent, where the parks are regarded by developers as a wasted space on the map.

'The South-East is done for,' she says, as we consider her options. 'But I can't be too far away or you won't visit me.'

The advantage of having a mother too far away to visit suddenly presents itself, but I say nothing.

'Of course,' she continues, 'what I really want is to go to the Amazon.'

'The Amazon. Really?'

We had difficulty getting her to spend a week in France last summer.

'Oh yes. I've always wanted to do that.'

She shoots me an accusing look, a look that says if it weren't for us she'd be living in a Yanomami longhouse, grinding manioc root and spearing fish.

'We probably wouldn't be able to come for weekends, though,' I say.

'No,' she says with a weird smile. 'You wouldn't.'

Before I was born she went round France with her boyfriend on his motorbike. And in the 1970s she went to Provence with three divorced friends, which technically is on the way to the Amazon. We start with a compromise: Dorset.

'Midge has a cottage there,' I remind her. Midge is my friend Claudia's mother. Her cottage is decorated with understated good taste, the way my life could be if I were someone else. It's not as breathtaking as the Brazilian rainforest but it's less than three hours' drive from London and there are cream teas.

Though Mum's house isn't even on the market yet, we are welcomed warmly by estate agents, who listen patiently to her requirements, which take up little time, and her denunciation of the government's plan to house half the population of Britain at the end of her road, which takes longer.

Our first viewing is of a house with a large garden that is almost totally wild. The owner, a good ten years older than my mother, is delighted to hear that she is also a keen gardener. As we go, she describes the various plants and shrubs: 'These are the roses, and here of course are the herbs – lavender, rosemary . . .'

She goes on in this vein, but there's just one problem: none of the plants she's naming are actually there. Mind you, I'm no gardener.

When we get back to the car, I say to Mum, 'Erm, were there seedlings or something that I couldn't see? All I could see was sort of long, dead grass.'

'No!' she says. 'There weren't any! She was completely imagining them!'

'Blimey.'

'Sssh, she's coming over!'

'One thing you should know,' says the woman. 'I'm in a bit of a dispute with the people next door over the rights to the paddock.'

Our next house has been photographed with not so much as a millimetre of space round it, causing us to wonder whether there just might possibly be something unsightly nearby. Sure enough, when we arrive we find a huge garage and tractor showroom right opposite, a row of particularly hideous new houses at the back and – the pièce de résistance – a series of rusting cars and caravans all over the garden. A gaggle of dark-haired, dirty children watch us warily as we knock on the door.

The woman owner shows us round, pointing out the DIY walls and ceilings they've put in – which appear to be made of polystyrene – and giving us a detailed history of her husband's indigestion. After about ten minutes my mother nudges me. The husband has appeared behind us and is silently following, while the wife is describing his various visits to the doctor, tests, stomach pains and so on, as if (a) we are doctors and (b) he isn't there. Mum and I know we absolutely cannot look at each other or we will be helpless. Once outside, we drive away quickly before we explode.

That night we stop in Dorchester and I leave her in the car while I go in and recce a B&B.

'Double or twin?' says the owner. 'The double has a four-poster.'

'Double please,' I say, knowing that a four-poster will be fun and anyway double rooms are usually nicer.

I go back out to get my mother and the luggage, and the woman looks at us oddly, as if something has changed.

'I think a twin,' she says firmly, her lips pressed together.

'What about the double?' I say.

'It's booked.'

Mum and I go up to the twin room and look at each other. We don't look at all alike and therefore don't appear to be related . . . Suddenly it dawns on us.

'She thinks we're gay!'

This unexpected manifestation of homophobia in Hardy Country has us in intermittent hysterics all the way through supper at a pub, after which we lie on our beds watching *Inspector Morse*. It also entertains us during the discovery that there are no charming old three-bedroom houses in my mother's price range in Dorset whatsoever. And so we plan a second trip, to Herefordshire.

'It's more rural,' she says. She knows someone with a cottage there too; her Russian friend Irena is away, but gives us directions and says we can use the cottage as a base from which to explore.

Herefordshire begins well. We go to see a house with oak beams on the edge of a common, which still holds the ancient grazing rights for one household: twenty-three sheep.

'I can have twenty-three sheep on the common,' she says.

'Mm,' I say. 'But can you park?'

After the hideous wrangles over parking at her current place, I am anxious for her to get a house which doesn't involve her having to rely on someone else's goodwill to reach her own front door.

The house on the common is promising. The outside is painted a very strange shade of orange – the same colour as some rice pudding my grandmother once made which made me sick – but apart from that it's fine. We have tea and cake with the vendor and leave feeling optimistic. On the way out, however, we get stuck in a ditch. A passing neighbour offers to fetch one of the local farmers to pull us out.

He arrives in a tractor and attaches a towrope.

'Don't pump the gas,' he instructs, 'or you'll flood it.'

Mum squeezes the accelerator gently but we don't move. The farmer gets out of his tractor to take a closer look and to offer encouragement.

'That's it, no, go on. Bit more.'

She keeps squeezing and we both look out at the farmer, who, as the back wheels spin, is being gradually covered all over with a fine coating of mud. As a spray-painting job it's excellent, but my mother is now laughing too hard to accelerate properly, and I'm no better. Eventually the car squelches suddenly backwards out of the mud like a baby being born and we thank the farmer, who drives away evidently oblivious of the mud, leaving us to laugh freely.

We go into Ludlow, the nearest town, to get some supplies for supper, and drive out to find Irena's cottage. I'm relieved it isn't for sale, as its lack of vehicle access – you have to park, then walk across a field – makes it dangerously appealing to my mother. When we get inside, though, we both gasp.

It's freezing and everything is covered in dust, dismally reminiscent of the cottage in *Withnail & I*, Bruce Robinson's comedy of 1960s squalor. A less welcoming billet would be hard to imagine.

'She obviously hasn't been here in a while,' says my mother, with commendable understatement.

We find a kettle and make tea. Suddenly she gasps again.

'A queen!'

'Eh?'

'Queen wasp. And another one! My God!'

'For God's sake, don't wake them up!'

All together we count six, all hibernating and all huge. Even my mother, with her interest in wildlife, is a bit taken aback.

'I've never seen that before,' she murmurs, as I pour the tea. There are clean mugs in a cupboard, but I can't find any heat source or even a fireplace and I know what we're both thinking: that with the cold, the dust and the wasps, this is both miserable and spooky and we should have checked it out earlier, i.e. before it got dark.

'We'll just have to lump it,' I say. 'Let's get the supper on, at least. That'll perk us up.'

But of the beautiful lamb chops we have bought there is no sign. We search everywhere, getting more and more baffled. Is there a carnivorous poltergeist? Ludlow is fifteen miles away, it's dark and a fine drizzle is faintly visible through the filthy windows. Neither of us feels like getting in the car again.

'Hell's bells,' she says. 'At least tell me we haven't lost the wine.'

One thing we agree on: we might, just, be able to cope in this place without food – but without a drink, no way.

We find the claret and – God be praised – a corkscrew. We drink up, then huddle without getting undressed beneath the damp, ancient duvet.

'My God!' she says in the dark, laughing. 'Billy Connolly once said that 80 per cent of all Scots people were conceived while their parents were fully clothed – and it's true!'

We shudder ourselves to sleep.

In the morning we have a mug of tea each, decide not to tangle with the long-dormant hot-water system and head unwashed for the car. As we're crossing the field, I notice a plastic carrier in the grass. It contains our chops, dropped unnoticed the night before and miraculously untouched by foxes.

'Och, well,' says my mother.

And we set off for the next house.

After a very enjoyable and entirely pointless few days, we return to Kent.

'Of course,' she says, 'what I really want is to live in a croft in the Hebrides.'

Seeing as we have just roughed it in Herefordshire and she wasn't too keen, I remain sceptical and she remains, for the moment, where she is. A few years later she does move, to another village in Kent about six miles away. The new village has a post office, a station, a free-range butcher and a general store. It lacks the wild beauty of the Hebrides, and indeed the mile-high vegetation, multicoloured birds and scantily attired, endangered indigenous peoples of the Amazon. But it is handier for weekends.

6 Love Frok Me

I am thirty. My grandmother dies, and my mother and I go up to Glasgow to make the arrangements. It is my first brush with the practical side of death.

When my grandfather died, I was twenty-two and still young enough to assume it was no big deal for her. She was getting on a bit, fifty-four by then, so I assumed it couldn't have been too bad. I was on holiday in America and came back to hear how she'd coped not just with the bereavement but with the far more challenging issue of her mother's state of mind.

'What are we doing today, Pat?' Granny would ask my mother, for the umpteenth time.

And my mother would answer, 'Daddy's funeral.'

Nine years on, my grandmother is gone too and I meet my mother at Euston. She hugs me and smiles; we're going to go on the train to Glasgow together, as we used to every summer, and some of the old holiday spirit pervades our mood. Is she feeling sad? I can't tell.

'It's quite an adventure,' she says, as we get beers and bacon sandwiches from the buffet car.

At Glasgow Central, though I know it's pointless, I can't help letting my eyes flick up the platform to look for the welcoming committee: Granny, Grandad and Uncle Charlie standing in a row, pinks from the garden in their buttonholes, saluting. Granny would be wearing a dress with matching jacket, usually either the pale turquoise or the navy, with a kind of ridging in the cloth. She'd have on her marquesite peacock brooch, because it was our favourite, and crimson lipstick from a time when you could only get two shades. She often wore her comedy smile, too. When she is long gone and I have children and many gaps in my memory, it is that smile which survives. Grandad would wear a white shirt, dark blue blazer and tie. He, or Uncle Charlie if he was absent, would finish the salute by uttering the traditional greeting: 'B – A – U!'

This stood for 'Beans Are Up!' – the runner beans they produced every August which towered above our heads with vivid red flowers in a great green screen. 'BAU' was also used by Granny to sign off her letters, along with the valediction which began as a slip of the hand at the typewriter and grew into a family catchphrase: Love Frok Me.

Is my mother remembering this too? We look at each other.

'B A U,' I say.

'B A U!' she says back.

From the station we'd make a grand progress through the city in Uncle Charlie's red Rover. Neither of the grandparents ever learned to drive, and this was one of the many ways in which he made himself indispensable. The night my grandfather brought him home for dinner, and he confessed to being miserable in his lodgings, my grandmother invited him to stay. He moved his books and pin-striped suits unobtrusively into the spare front bedroom and was transformed from my grand-father's colleague into Uncle Charlie. My grandpar-ents had lost Neil, their first child, and the whole family seemed to benefit from his presence, like a sick body with a heart transplant. What my mother could never understand was how such a lovely man remained single.

But there is no welcoming committee, no red Rover, of course. So we get into a taxi, and my mother does her usual thing of asking the driver about his part of the city, telling him where she was born – Langside – and explaining that she's a south-erner now, has been for forty years. But her accent has come back since we got off the train. I look out of the window at the still-grubby city, for it has not yet become City of Culture and been cleaned up. Somewhere in those red sandstone streets is the cinema where we saw *The Wizard of Oz* and the trattoria where, aged seven, I had my first *pollo sorpresa* and the waiter poured my Coca-Cola with a flourish, saying it was champagne.

In no time at all we're out in the lush suburbs, smelling the pines. Giffnock, on the south side, is still as full of roses as when I was a child. Our B&B is near the rose-flanked path that my sister and I used to run up to get to the shops, competing to be first to make it through the gate at the end. I am expecting everything to chime with my rosy memory of the place, so it comes as a bit of a jolt to find that our hosts are not part of this. I put our bags on the armchair in our room and immediately the owner, Mrs McCready, rushes in. Perhaps she's been spying on us through a hole in the wall.

'We've got family staying here next week!' she admonishes, shoving the bags on to the floor. Why do people who don't like strangers in the house run B&Bs? When she's gone my mother makes a rude face.

The following morning at breakfast I politely

refuse her offer of a sausage with my egg and bacon. I'm not really a sausage person.

'But I've already started cooking it!' she complains. My mother looks down at her tea, smirking. This is all part of the adventure. Awful people bring us together, schoolkids united against a ghastly teacher.

The hospital where Granny spent her last months is a bus ride away, followed by a walk across a windswept housing estate of the sort featured in news reports with headlines like 'Deprived Britain', or, if in the *Daily Mail*, 'Britain on the Fiddle'. Instead of being crammed together, though, the squat, chunky tower blocks are spaced far apart on a treeless expanse of patchy grass like an urban moor. Apparently unaffected by the surrounding bleakness, my mother strolls along cheerily.

'Of course, this is what the Scots would call a lovely sunny day,' she says.

The geriatric ward scares me. I stand very still, trying not to breathe in or touch anything, while my mother chats happily to the sister as if at a do.

'Where is she now? Have the men been, from the Co-op?'

'Oh, aye, they've been and collected her this morning, uh-huh,' says the sister.

'I do want to thank you for looking after her,' she says.

'Och, not at all.'

It is not a myth that the Scots say 'och'.

'Do you have a staff social fund?'

My mother writes out a cheque for £100 for the nurses and a second one for the 'Ash Cash', the £25 perk paid to the certificating medic in cases of cremation. Having lived with a doctor, she knows all about this.

'He came every day, you know,' says another nurse. 'Mr Duncan.'

'He'd just sit in the chair, holding her hand,' adds the sister.

'Aye.'

My mother nods. Mr Duncan is of course 'Uncle Charlie'. I do not know it yet, but – just in time, before it is too late – my mother is piecing things together.

Uncle Charlie has been moved to a sheltered flat and the house has already been sold, by Aunt Valerie, from whom we have strict instructions to empty it completely. The front garden is still full of roses, and the green-painted low wooden fence of uprights and Xs, like a string of Roman numerals, looks just the same. Each house has a different colour fence to match its paintwork, so you can pick out the green one from the top of the street.

'We came to watch this being built,' says my mother. 'Saw it marked out on the ground.'

'1932 was it?'

'That's right. I was four.'

If as a child I had drawn the perfect grandparents' house with my many sets of pencils, it could not have been more ideal. Set back from the road behind a generous front garden and enclosed by its green fence, it was, because so unlike our flat in London, utterly exotic.

The first thing we always saw, coming into the hall, was the Bakelite telephone on its special fitted cupboard by the front door, in keeping with the British tradition of having to be both cold and standing when taking a call. Beyond that was the green trough of feathery pink astilbe, like an indoor window box but on the floor, and against the back wall the 'grandmother' clock. Uncle Charlie had made this himself and its quarter-hour chimes were as vital to the house as a heartbeat. Against the other side wall were always a sack or two of silver milk-bottle tops, which, Granny said, were to be turned into Guide Dogs for the Blind. It was never explained to us how this was done.

A man from an auction house is going to come later to look at the better pieces of furniture. Everything else that he can't sell or that we don't want will be taken by the house-clearance men. When we go in, however, my mother notices that someone else has already started the job.

'Oh my God!' she gasps in the doorway of the dining room. 'The green ladies have gone!'

The green ladies are a pair of Art Deco statuettes which have sat on the mantelpiece since she was a child. She tries the door handle of the French windows leading to the back garden and finds them unlocked.

'D'you think they've been burgled?' I say.

'Uh-uh. I'm afraid it's Mrs Grey.'

Every time she or Valerie has been up, something from the house, something antique and portable, has always been missing. And Mrs Grey, the home help, has always been off sick. One of the absent items is a china toby jug which shared the mantelpiece with the green ladies, and which my mother was scared of as a child. My sister and I, too, feared its shiny, grimacing face. When we came, Granny would impatiently turn its creepy features to the wall, sighing that we were 'just as silly as Pat'. Now it's gone, and my mother says, 'Well, at least we won't miss it!'

You have to hand it to her for not being materialistic.

'Well! Let's start with a cup of tea,' she says, and we go in and put on the kettle.

My sister and I loved our Scottish holidays. When we came to stay, our mother usually shared with Granny, getting one of the twin beds with their luxurious rustly counterpanes. These were white lace over pale green silky stuff, and matched the curtains on the glass-topped dressing table which we coveted intensely. Opposite that was the wardrobe where she kept her dresses and her fox-fur stole, and lots of pairs of stockings in very thin boxes. In the small, tiled fireplace there was an electric fire which was never switched on, even when there were frost flowers on the windows, and on the narrow, stepped mantelpiece, two sitting china ladies in mauve dresses with frilled white petticoats showing underneath. My sister and I preferred these to the more valuable green ladies in the living room because of their frills. On arrival we would always run our gaze over the wall to check that they were all there, and that on the table between the beds there was still the little pile of books full of cartoons about monks. With everything as it should be, we would run out to play.

Grandad would have already moved upstairs to the attic room which used to be the maid's, giving us his room, the back bedroom which was the exact opposite of Granny's: dark, with a double bed covered with a dark green quilt – no lace – that used to slide off when we turned over in the night. Apart from that there was a wardrobe, a plain wooden dressing table where he kept his bottle of Old Spice and the two rectangular brushes for the sides of his head which still had hair, and on the wall, a map of Islay, the whisky-distilling island home of his branch of the McNeills.

Strangely, it seems to me now, for someone who grew up in poverty and through two wars, Granny spoiled us massively. In the mornings she brought us breakfast in bed, boiled eggs on trays – one each – with an embroidered tray cloth and a slim glass containing one of Grandad's precious pinks from the garden. My mother, who'd always been 'chivvied' as a child to hurry up and get on, must have been astonished. If Granny and Charlie had been out to play bridge the night before, there'd also be two small, brown envelopes containing their winnings: third prize 2/6, second 5/- or, best of all, first prize, which was 7/6. This satisfyingly heavy clutch of coins bought several comics, a toy or two and a quarter of iced caramels at the confectioner's – even more if Mum's back was turned. These were flattish cubes of fudgy toffee covered in crunchy pink or white icing. We ate the white ones first and saved the pink, even though they tasted the same.

If there were no bridge winnings, which was rare, one of them would beckon us solemnly towards them, saying, 'There's a picture of the Queen for each of you on the mantelpiece,' and we would run over to find a pound note each, or, on one extravagant occasion, two fivers.

Granny's 'dream kitchen', of tall white metal cupboards and red and white checked lino, had a table in the middle with a huge Kenwood mixer on it which produced slightly grim lunches of mince and boiled potatoes or whiting, fried – not very crisply, in her own batter. Occasionally we suffered Uncle Charlie's 'burgers', made from mince, sausage-meat, fresh yeast – we never discovered why – and tomato ketchup.

Claire, being more of a strategist than I, would manage to get in first with, 'Sorry, I'm not very hungry today,' leaving my mother and me to soldier on through the vaguely meat-like slabs. In ironic deference to our accents, he pronounced them *'berh-gers'*, stretching down his upper lip to perfect the strange English vowels.

Meals were issued from a hatch in the kitchen-dining-room wall, which my sister and I loved to open and shut over and over again, listening out for the 'clack' as the doors closed together and poking our heads through to 'surprise' the grown-ups. We could never see why they weren't as entertained by this ritual as we were.

After lunch we could go out through the dining-room French windows and into the big, L-shaped garden – huge by London standards, with its vegetable patch and lawn fringed by roses and pinks, grown by my grandfather, which looked like miniature carnations, but with flat petals instead of frilly, and smelled magically of vanilla. There were clear lines of demarcation in the garden. Grandad grew the flowers and Uncle Charlie the peas and beans; Granny stayed out of their way. Behind the back fence was the long, thin wood, which stretched behind the back gardens all the way up the road, so you could go out of the back door, through the gap in the fence, through the wood, out the top and all the way back down the street to the house. We were obsessed with circuits. Instead of this one, or if it was raining, we'd go out the back door, through the shrubbery at the side by the garage and – Granny wasn't so keen on this one – in through the front bedroom window. Or we could walk down to the playground at the end of the street, which was a cul-de-sac, and go on the swings until tea.

High tea was also eaten in the light dining room at the dark, square, wooden table with lace cloth. Since we had no such meal at home, this was doubly looked forward to: tinned ham, cucumber, tomatoes, bread and butter, home-made drop scones, slim honeycomb bars – not Crunchies – and Tunnock's teacakes, chocolate-covered marshmallows on little biscuit bases. The jam and Rose's lime marmalade were served in faceted green glass dishes. It was lucky none of us drank tea, since any left over from the previous meal was reheated in the oven still in the pewter pot with its pocked surface reminiscent of a freshly cemented path after rain. Later, as a teenager, my sister made Grandad a pot of fresh tea of such a rich brown colour that he didn't recognize it as a distant relation of the greyish liquid he had been drinking all those years.

Once during the week we'd have a bath, in the most exotic room of all, black and green with a round window like the stateroom on a liner. Granny had asked specifically for a round window when the house was being built; she felt it was the epitome of opulence. We'd sit in the water, wrinkling up our noses at the smell of the Wright's Coal Tar soap – never was a soap named so determinedly in defiance of the need for sales – and trying to generate some lather. The swankiness of the bathroom was only slightly undermined by a roll of hard Izal lavatory paper, occasionally replaced by squares of newspaper when it ran out.

So as not to waste the cartridge drawing pad she always has in her bag, my mother has brought some scrap paper with which to label everything 'Keep', 'Sell' or 'Out'. I am allowed to keep Granny's pink and green jug and matching scallop-edged lemonade glasses, which are still in the glass sideboard in the sitting room, and for my sister, the deep blue glass sundae dishes and single green and silver cocktail glass with a bobble on its stem.

'Oh, and look at this!'

It's an Edward VIII coronation mug.

'For the coronation that never was! It could be valuable.'

'Not very,' says my mother. 'I'm afraid it's chipped.'

I decide to keep it anyway.

When the auction man arrives, they disappear into Uncle Charlie's room. At the sheltered housing, he only has space for his bed, armchair and clock. His rattan three-seater with its distinctive back like three circles stuck together has had to stay behind. While they discuss its potential value, if any, I linger in Grandad's room, gazing out at the garden through the sun porch.

'Only an insane optimist would build a sun porch north of the border,' my mother used to joke, but in summer it did store heat, making it warmer than the rest of the house. It ran the width of the back bedroom but without a connecting door and therefore couldn't be used for a circuit. So Claire and I would go outside to get into it, climb on to two of the three canvas folding chairs that sat in a row facing the lawn, hold the position for about ten seconds and then go out again. This way we always succeeded in experiencing every room in the house.

After the auction man has gone, with a shorter list than my mother had hoped, the clearance men arrive, three of them, all short and wiry. My mother makes them a cup of tea and rolls her eyes at me.

'Very "rough types",' she says. 'Look at their teeth. Or the lack of them.'

True, they don't look like the sort of men either of us would want to be left alone with, but together, in our team of two, we are cheerful and confident. She takes them briefly into each room, pointing out the pieces of paper taped to the furniture and, just in case their literacy skills aren't on a par with ours, casually reciting the words on each.

'We've put our own things in this corner,' she explains, indicating our coats and bags. She evidently knows how thorough they are going to be.

She and I linger in the kitchen, then in the hall, then in the kitchen again. The men pick up the scratchy green armchairs from the living room and heft them on to their lorry with what seems minimal effort. After a while their boss arrives, a slim quiet man from the council. He takes my mother off into the garden with what appears to be something important to discuss. I wander back into Grandad's room to see one of the men trying on my mother's jacket.

'Oh! That's not going,' I say. 'It was in that pile, see?'

'Oh, right, hen,' he says neutrally, and takes it off.

I feel pleased at having handled the moment

coolly, but also a bit edgy inside, like someone who's seen behind the door of an operating theatre and wishes they hadn't.

The men are nearly finished. I can hear them discussing whether they can fit Granny's wardrobe on to the lorry and deciding they can't. I want to keep it, along with the dressing table, but my mother has already reminded me that they're not that lovely really, and that anyway there is no room. In the time it takes me to regret this, they have smashed the wardrobe apart with a hammer and begun to load the pieces on to the lorry. The violence of it is shocking. When my mother and the man from the council come back in I wait to hear what the important thing was he had to discuss with her and find that there doesn't seem to have been one. Either it's lucky chance or he has deliberately kept her in the garden to spare her what I've just seen.

At the end of the day, high on our own efficiency, we go up the road for a curry and back to the B&B. Speculating about what punishment might ensue if we wake Mrs McCready, we giggle as we tiptoe up the stairs.

The Co-op funeral home is on the main road, a few doors down from the chippy and the sweet shop where we used to buy our iced caramels. We collect

Uncle Charlie from his sheltered flat and Valerie and my sister arrive from down south. Granny is last. We all sit in the black car while we wait for the hearse. I can't help noticing that one of the funeral directors is young and extremely good-looking.

I point this out to my mother, who whispers, 'Ah, maybe he gets to "comfort" a lot of widows.'

The hearse seems to take ages. After about ten minutes Uncle Charlie says he needs the loo. The funeral home's vehicle entrance faces a parking area at the back of the block shared with the adjacent shops and – as we're about to discover – the bottle banks. As Charlie reaches for the door handle and attempts to get out of the car, someone drops a couple of wine bottles into the nearest one, about six feet away from us, and he falls back into his seat. I hope the shock won't kill him.

'What was that?'

'It's all right, Charlie,' says my mother. 'It's just someone putting something in the bottle bank.'

'The bank?'

Charlie spent his career in banks – it was where he met my grandfather – and I can see the concern on his face as he struggles to remember assessing loan applications to the sound of smashing glass.

'It's not really a bank,' says my mother. 'It's more

of a large container. They take the bottles away and melt them down and make them into new ones.'

'Aye, well, I think I do need to go right enough,' he says, and my mother gets out of the car to find out where to take him. But it's obvious, to her at least, that he's going to need some help. To our immense relief, two of the Co-op funeral staff come out with her, gently take Charlie by one arm each and steer him back inside. Through the open back door I can see that they've gone all the way into the Gents itself. Are they helping him with the zip and associated manoeuvres? We all look at each other and then away. I'm afraid they're going to come back out and say something about this not being included in the package, but they deposit him carefully back in the car and tell us we won't have long to wait long now.

We chat on quietly in the back of the car, pausing for the smashing of bottles, and eventually see the coffin being brought out and loaded into the hearse. It's accompanied by a very short, extremely old man who gets into the driver's seat of our car.

'He's not the driver?!' says Valerie in a stage whisper. 'He looks ready to keel over himself.'

As he gets in, and sinks so far down he can barely see over the steering wheel, we have to look away from each other because we're starting to giggle.

The crematorium is as municipally soulless as these civic departure lounges tend to be, but our ceremony has something to distinguish it. After a quick burst of 'Jesu, Joy of Man's Desiring', which my mother requests on the grounds that all organists know it, I stand at the lectern to read some extracts from Granny's letters. I feel self-conscious reading to so small an audience, but forget all this when I hear the poem my mother has written.

She takes my place on the low platform and says, 'Here are a few verses about Lizzie, written when she had started to float away from us, in her eighties:

She was a circus, a fair and a playground
She threw us down raisins from two storeys up
The biscuits you liked she made till you hated them
She sang like a bass till you begged her to stop.

Whistled as sweetly as chaps who get paid for it
Played the piano by ear and by feel
Said about writing she thought she was made for it
She was better than books, for her stories were real.

Her eye was as sharp and as blue as a jaybird's
It never shed tears for her childhood or such
No cash for the bottle of ink for her homework,
She mixed soot and water and made a brave botch.

She questioned believers but sang all the psalm tunes
She crossed swords with priests and she argued with God
And folk still remember their pleasure to be there,
For the tea, and the fun, and the talking they had.

For she was a theatre, forum and cockpit
Now in her eighties a playhouse gone dark.
And dark is the mind that was rainbow and rocket
And I am the bird that flew out of her ark.

Afterwards we have lunch at a recently opened restaurant serving traditional Scottish food in trendy, pale-wood surroundings, something Granny would not have been able to imagine. Mum's wealthy cousin, Granny's nephew, does not offer to contribute. His brother, the other cousin, who has health problems, says, 'Very kind of you, Pat,' and leaves before everyone else, moving out of the door and taking very small steps down the street, as if holding on to what life he has left.

We take Uncle Charlie back to his sheltered flat and Mum sits with him for a while. We are back down south before she tells me that she has finally asked him the question which has been in the back of her mind for a long time: if he is her father.

'But you look exactly like your dad!' I say. 'The McNeill nose!'

It has a very slightly flat bit on the end. It's unique to the McNeills and Lydia has it too.

'I know, I know,' she says. 'I just used to wish he was.'

She has few really positive memories of her father and from quite an early age invested her admiration in Charlie, who introduced her to natural history, which, along with drawing, became her great passion. It was he who encouraged her to travel, gave her tips on etiquette and, when he was transferred to the bank's prestigious Regent Street office in London, took her out to lunch as fathers should.

'What did he say when you asked him?' I say finally.

'He said, "Oh no, the dates were wrong."'

We look at each other.

'So now we know.'

'He adored her. All those years I thought he was gay or a secret transvestite! He was staying there to be near my mother.'

'I guess there are only so many plots,' I say. 'What about your father? Do you feel sorry for him?'

'Oh, I think he made other arrangements. He was very handsome and charming to women, you know. I remember noticing that for a bank manager he didn't leave much money in his will, and at his funeral there were two women I'd never seen before, weeping copiously.'

For her this is as good as case closed.

7 Bride's Mother Revisited

I've got the photographs of my parents' wedding and only one of my grandmothers is in them. My father's mother is there, her shoulders high and chest pushed up, like a general. My mother's father is there. But my mother's mother was back in Glasgow. The only reason my mother could give was what Granny had told her on the phone: 'She said there didn't seem much point coming all that way as it was only a register office.'

Recently Mum told me she didn't think her mother had forgiven her for rejecting a rich suitor she didn't love. Yet she travelled the 390 miles to London the day after for the reception, which made her absence even more baffling. Still, I shoved it to the back of my mind and never thought that, when my turn came, my mother might be a bit peculiar about weddings too.

Pretty much everyone I knew or heard about who'd got married had suffered the over-attentions of their mothers. The traditional scenario involved being trapped for hours in meticulous discussions about seating plans and the colour of the bridesmaids' ribbons while the men around them were shut out, so that eventually the day seemed to be about the bride's mother, with everyone else, including the groom, relegated to bit parts. Some, pushed beyond endurance, bailed out. Peter's friend Meg escaped by going to Venice. My friend Sarah and her chap went to Antigua. She came back to a mother who wasn't speaking to her, but she, and particularly he, felt it was worth it.

I didn't have to go anywhere. When we told my mother the good news, she said, 'That's wonderful!'

Then her interest kind of waned.

Deprived of any discussions about seating plans and bridesmaids' ribbons – not that we were actually having bridesmaids – I realized I desperately wanted some. My sister, for whom no detail is too trivial, rose to the occasion with relish. And Peter, unusually for his gender, caught the mood and became just as obsessed as we were about who should sit with whom. The three of us wrote the names of the guests on pieces of paper, spread them on the floor of his flat and spent days rearranging them into every conceivable combination, like Consequences. It was great fun. But I still wanted my mother to be a bit more – well, *engaged*.

'Look on the bright side,' said Peter, on the first of what were to be many occasions. 'It leaves us free to have the wedding we want.'

'Yeah, I know.'

'I mean, think of all the people who haven't had the wedding they wanted.'

'I know.'

'Like that girl you worked with: her mother took over the guest list and wouldn't let her have her own friends. Remember? And made the bridesmaids wear orange.'

'Apricot.'

'Whatever.'

'I know.'

'Or did I ever tell you about Tessa?'

'Who was Tessa?' I knew that he was trying to talk me out of my position on this, but I was none-theless curious.

'She was one of the people I shared a house with. She married an American. His mother got so into the idea of an English wedding, she hired Castle Howard.'

'No way!'

Castle Howard isn't just *any* stately home. It's where they filmed *Brideshead Revisited*.

'His mother took over the whole thing, with the castle and the posh caterers and thousands of pounds' worth of florists and so on. But *her* mother was just a normal Yorkshirewoman. She got so freaked out by the Castle Howard thing she had her entire house redecorated.'

'Not really?'

'She got completely stressed out and five weeks after the wedding she was dead.'

'Oh my God . . .'

'So, I'm just saying that we are, you know, really lucky here.'

'Really, really lucky, I know. I *know!*'

And he was right. One thing we'd always agreed on was that we wouldn't have apricot bridesmaids. Or any bridesmaids. Or pageboys. Or embossed ivory invitations. Or morning dress. Or the 'Wedding March'. Or a 'top table'. Or a wedding list full of preposterous items like *silver plated spoon rest*. Or anyone there we didn't really, really like. With Peter's parents both being dead, we had no interference from his side. So a mother with no interest in the preparations should have been absolutely ideal.

If there was anyone who probably *would* have filled the role of Bride's Parent from Hell it was my father. When he heard the good news you could almost see him start rehearsing his role, the marriage of his first-born an event at which he could *preside*. But that winter he died and so we never got to find out how annoying he might have been. We thought of cancelling, but Peter felt that in our grief we needed the wedding even more. We decided instead to acknowledge the death as part of the ceremony and went ahead.

As we divided up all the things that needed to be done, my mother offered to perform two tasks, which were to design the order of service cards – she was a demon with Letraset* – and order the flowers. The cards turned out beautifully. But something rather strange came over her when she got to the flowers.

Our colour scheme, based on my dress, was red. Near my mother's village there was a lady who did flowers – so all my mother had to do was tell her the colour and she would get whatever was in season and there would be displays in that colour in the church, reception room and dining room, and that

* Rub-down lettering used by designers pre-computers.

would be that. No white, no pink, no purple: just red.

As the big day drew nearer, she took to ringing me periodically with what she evidently thought to be updates, which went like this: 'Hello, this is just to say that the flowers are all In Hand.'

'Oh. Thanks. That's great. Is there anything – do you – is there . . . anything else?'

Her voice would then assume a slightly mechanical tone, as if she were reading from a card.

'I'm saying: the flowers are all In Hand.'

Then about two weeks before the Day, she said, 'There's a problem with your having red. Well, it's not a problem at all actually. You just won't be able to have red.'

'What?'

I had by this point been to see samples of the actual flowers we were having.

'The girl who's getting married after you, her father also died recently and they had red flowers at the funeral, so she'd prefer not to have red.'

'She doesn't have to. I'm the one having red, not her.'

'No, no. You haven't understood. She can't have red flowers in the church because it will upset her, and her wedding's right after yours, so she'd like you to have white.'

'I'm not having white. I don't give a fuck what she wants. I'm paying and I'm having red.'

'Well, what am I to tell her?'

'Try this: *My daughter is having red.*'

'Well, you've put me in a very awkward position.'

'I don't fucking care!'

It was pretty obvious she'd agreed without even asking me. I hung up.

Then a few days before the Day, my mother offered to perform one further task, which was to take the Dress to be pressed. It had travelled 12,000 miles from Australia, where we had bought it, and so was, unsurprisingly, somewhat creased.

'Let's do it two days before, though,' I said, 'just, you know, in case.'

Not long before, another bride in the village had sent her dress to be pressed and it hadn't come back in time. She had to go up the aisle in her sister's beige suit.

'You can absolutely have my blue silk if, you know, anything *happens*,' said my sister.

And I said, 'Thanks!' thinking that whatever happened I didn't want to be married in blue, which was always her colour, but in red, which was mine. Besides, the dress had come this far.

On the Thursday, therefore, my mother duly collected the Dress and it was Not Pressed.

'Mum – this hasn't been pressed. Look.'

'Yes, it has.'

'No, look. All the same creases are there, in exactly the same places. They've obviously forgotten to do it.'

'No, no. It's fine.'

'No, LOOK. They've clearly *not done it*, and put it on the "done" rail by mistake. It has to go back.'

'I've shown it to Joan, who used to be a dress-maker. And she says it's fine.'

My mother has always had a sort of panel of experts in her life, or perceived experts, who claim superiority of knowledge in all matters. I once popped my head round the door to say I was going out to get a book and she gestured extravagantly at her guest, a man with a domed forehead who organized science fiction conventions.

'If it's books you want,' she proclaimed, 'here's your man!'

He and I looked at each other for a moment.

'It's for French Lit,' I muttered, and slid out the door.

Joan was a more recent incumbent, who had been accorded top expert status.

'Listen to me,' I said. 'I don't give a shit what she thinks. She's not getting married in it. *I am*. If I don't get sent to prison for murdering you first.'

Had she really taken the dress round to show her? And if there was nothing wrong with it, *why*?

'Well, there's clearly no reasoning with you,' she concluded.

I phoned the dry-cleaner's in Canterbury.

'Oh dear, that's terrible,' said the owner. 'I will have it collected right now and bring it back to you tomorrow morning – personally.'

And he did.

When I was four, I was so convinced my mother valued other people more than me that when I came home from school one day to find a brand-new party dress on my bed, I asked her if it was for Nicky, my best friend. She was astonished, had genuinely never preferred another child to me. Yet when friends – guests, anyone – came into her orbit they did exert a stronger gravitational pull. Even my first school was chosen by a man she knew slightly, whom she invested with special insight into the education system. He recommended it highly; his own children were doing marvellously there. He neglected to mention that the woman who ran it was mad.

That night, she appeared with a blue garter and held it out reverently. I wouldn't have been surprised to hear it accompanied by celestial singing.

'Joan gave me this for you. She'd like you to wear it.'

'Er . . . why?'

Joan had struck again! She was not an old family friend. She had never held me on her knee or babysat me or slept with my father or been there through any of our major life events. I had never seen the garter as a child and thought, *Whatever happens, one day I must get married in that*. Yet here my mother was, holding it out to me. As with the flowers, I just knew she'd already agreed.

'Something Borrowed, Something Blue. You know.'

'I'm not doing that, though, am I? I'm not even that sort of person.'

'But – she's lent it to me for you.'

'*I'm not wearing it*. I don't wear garters or stockings or any of that stuff; I never have. It's blue and the dress is *red*. And anyway it's horrible.'

'But what shall I tell her?'

'I don't give a flying fuck what you tell her. I'm not wearing it.'

I went to bed.

'You did want her to take more of an interest in the wedding,' said Peter, as he tried to snuggle against my back.

'Fuck off, you traitor,' I explained. 'I'm not marrying you now anyway.'

The next night, the one before the Day, I heard the bell-ringers practising and went down to the church to have a listen and to experience a last moment of singleness. The July sun was glinting off the weathervane, spicy aromas were wafting over the green from the curry house and the scene was perfect. I slipped into the church and paused, thinking of all the couples who had stood there before us.

Then the door closed behind me, at which I discovered it had a lock on it like the front door of a house, only on the wrong side. I was locked in. I repeatedly pressed a button on the wall at the side of the door, desperately hoping it would make a sound that could be heard – somewhere. I couldn't help noticing the symbolism; so far, not being married was proving to be far more confining than being married. Eventually the bell-ringers paused, heard whatever sound was emanating from the button and, unimpressed by the depths of my gratitude, came down and let me out.

'Thank you, thank you, THANK YOU,' I gushed. 'I mean, you know, I didn't want to have to break one of these twelfth-century windows!'

They looked at me for a moment, and one of them said, 'Actually it dates from the threenth century, but the steeple and chancel were rebuilt in the 1700s.'

'Right. Great!'

'Well, see you tomorrow then,' they said, and went back to their belfry.

Peter and I walked up the aisle together, to Prokofiev's 'March of the Capulets'. I wished we'd had a practice run; the rhythm was so slow that trying to keep step with each other was something of a challenge. We'd wondered about doing an IRA funeral-type march, pausing with each step, or just walking normally, and as the dilemma hadn't been resolved by kick-off, we ended up doing a bit of both.

The contrast between the sunny churchyard and the dark interior enhanced the charged atmosphere, and when I appeared in my red dress – with black veil – there was a definite hush. The friends I had told about the veil thought it in dubious taste, and

Peter's stepmother was doubtless pursing her lips. At least I hoped so. My sister read out a sonnet she'd written for Dad, the service was punctuated by rather more pronounced snuffling than is usual at weddings, and when we emerged into the sun again there was a definite sense of catharsis.

The red flowers on the ends of the pews were gathered up and removed, so the other bereaved bride never had to see them and our friends had mementoes to take home. Shea, my old nanny, put hers on her husband's grave, connecting him to us, and the past to the future.

My mother gave an excellent speech which quoted from a Victorian book of etiquette and made no reference to the number and character of Peter's predecessors, my lack of restraint at the champagne table or any of the other topics people traditionally find amusing when they make speeches at weddings.

It was only afterwards, when we got the pictures back, that we found she wasn't in them. Agreeing that we both disliked formal posed shots, we did some in couples, families and small groups. Then, when we were all having drinks in the beautiful old college courtyard, someone had the idea of going up on to the balcony overlooking it to take an overhead shot of everyone together. In the excitement I failed to notice that my mother had chosen that moment to go to the loo.

So that was how my wedding pictures ended up without my mother in them, just like hers.

'I can't believe she did that,' I told Peter, when we finally got back to my mother's house after shaking off a guest who was too drunk to find her room and asked if she could stay with us.

'We could have stood around for hours lined up in various permutations,' he reminded me. 'We chose not to. Don't worry: I got some pictures of her.'

'Just not with everybody else.'

'The point is, it was a fantastic day. And anyway, everyone was looking at *you*.'

'In a good way, right?'

'I'm not going to answer that,' he said, and went to sleep.

8 East of Swiss Cottage
and South of Reason

It's the 1990s. Peter and I are married and in our first house, no children yet. Life is relatively simple. My mother is staying with us for five days while she goes on a course. It's a personal development or 'self-improvement' course, although she's indicated she doesn't need any such thing. But I've done it and several of our friends – the definitely not crazy ones – have done it, and so she is going to break out of character and follow the crowd.

We live in Islington and the course is in Swiss Cottage, two areas both in north London but unconnected by public transport. She has been offered a lift by someone else on the course. They'll be passing through our bit of Islington, or at least King's Cross, which is nearby, and they can drop her off. The afternoon before the first day of the course she asks me for the directions to our house to give them. It's a sunny day and we're standing in the front garden.

'It's quite simple,' I say. 'We're to the east of the course centre, so—'

'The east?' she says. 'But you told me you live in north London.'

'We do. We're east of Swiss Cottage. So anyway—'

'So why are you telling me to go east?'

'Because that's the direction of travel. OK, never mind east. The easiest way is for them to get to Camden Town, then cross Agar Grove, taking Brewery Road.'

'What's Brewery Road?'

'It's a road. It leads from Camden Town to the road just up there: Caledonian Road.'

'So now you want us to take Caledonian Road? This is very confusing.'

'No, it's not. Really. It's a series of roads, not one or the other. I'll do you a map.'

I start the map, but when I look up to re-establish eye contact, she's rolling her eyes upwards, like Stevie Wonder.

'Here, down here,' I say. 'Look at the map.'

'I can't focus on maps, I'm sorry.'

'Why?'

'They remind me of my father.'

'This isn't about your father; it's about getting from Swiss Cottage to Islington.'

In case you're wondering, my mother didn't have a dark childhood experience involving maps. She wasn't abused by her father in a map-lined room, for instance. Nor was she beaten by him in Stanfords, the famous map shop, or abandoned as a baby on the steps of the Royal Geographical Society. She has suffered no harm in her life whatsoever, directly or indirectly, caused by maps. Nonetheless she continues to stare pointedly upwards, as if my diagram is emitting evil death rays.

'For God's sake, will you look at the bloody map!'

'Now you're doing exactly what he used to do.'

I may well be, and I have some sympathy for the man. He did survive the horrors of the First World War after all. She says that that was no excuse, however, for his habit of interrupting whatever she was doing – writing poetry, gazing at trees – to fire questions at her: 'What's the highest mountain in the world? Longest river in Africa?' And so on. Thus my mother, a dreamy, imaginative child, was given a lifelong fear of facts. She even claimed he would lurk behind doors and jump out at her, barking these questions and trying, she says, to catch her out.

So what we have here is a sort of knowledge-aversion syndrome. She knows lots of stuff. She just can't absorb information from someone with whom she's emotionally involved. I used to think she hated having anything explained to her by *my* father because she was married to him. But now I realize we all turn into *her* father the minute we try to explain anything. Abstract facts are OK, like 'Oranges contain more Vitamin C than chairs'. But information relating to her daily life, like how to get from A to B, let alone C, cannot penetrate. She emits a mental fog, like a cornered animal, and nothing can get through. And directions are the worst. They get rejected by her mental antibodies like a foreign kidney.

'Look,' I say, 'why don't you just give this to the person driving you?'

But she won't look at it.

'OK, well – then I just don't know how you're going to get back, really.'

'You could tell me how, instead of attacking me.'

'I'm *trying* to tell you; you won't let me!'

'That's ridiculous! Who's stopping you?'

'You! You won't *listen*!'

'You have this idea that people aren't listening to you. That's paranoid.'

Now she's got her invisible-psychiatrist coat on, where I'm in the cardigan that does up at the back and she's diagnosing me.

'Look, the course is *here*. We live *here*. OK? Just get them to drive to King's Cross, then back up again. That involves the fewest turns. Or they could use the *A–Z*!'

I indicate, in what I hope is an un-her-father-like way, the general sweep of the route.

'You haven't mentioned Essex Road.'

'I'm sorry?'

'When do we turn into Essex Road?'

'You don't. It's the other side.'

'What do you mean, "the other side"?'

She repeats 'the other side' as if I've said 'add two pounds of flour'.

'It's the other side of here from Swiss Cottage. You don't go near it.'

'You're not making sense, I'm afraid. I'm just asking when we get to Essex Road.'

'You *don't*! It's *that way*!'

'Well, why include it then?'

'I *DIDN'T*!'

'You were the one who mentioned the Essex Road.'

'*When?*'

'Oh, surely I don't have to give dates and times?'

She laughs. Now we've gone from incredulous shrink to SS officer telling escaped POW, '*For you, the war is over.*'

'Look, can we just forget about Essex Road?'

'Fine by me. You're the one who brought it up.'

The mobile phone has been invented and soon everyone will have one, and I will be able to speak to the people bringing back my mother and not have a nervous breakdown. In the meantime, I am going to try not to kill her.

At about eleven p.m. on the first day of the course, she rings the doorbell.

'So you got here OK?'

'Yes,' she says. 'It was quite simple, not as you said at all. Why did you make it so complicated?'

9 The Mental Elf

I pressed the alarm button in a lift once. My therapist said it was a cry for help.

Well, *der*.

I was rescued by firemen, who pushed the lift back from its position stuck between my accountant's floor and the one below, and realigned it. I wish that could happen more in life, not because firemen are attractive, though they often are, but because it would be so useful. You'd ring the emergency number, tell them your life has got stuck between two outcomes – for example, you're neither contentedly married with children nor happily single, just drifting and miserable – and they'd come round with the equipment to push it back on course. They could be like the Robert de Niro character who swings into the apartment in *Brazil*: Buttle, or was it Tuttle. I like the sense that when the authorities won't help you, there's a loner operating outside the system, a maverick who knows how things really work. When

I first got Broadband and it didn't work, I had to plug into an underground network of people who fix these things. I started with a guy of indeterminate origin, Indian Ocean islander possibly, who sorted out the wiring, then he gave me the number for a Cypriot guy who fixed the actual Broadband. The Cypriot guy was here for three hours and I paid him forty pounds, which was almost certainly cheaper than holding on waiting for BT to answer their helpline.

When I was small there was an aura of mystery attached to Tom the Gas, the retired fitter who mended Ascots – those metal boxes with unsealed flues that belched out lethal fumes while they heated the water. My mother said it was very important never to ask him anything personal – such as his surname – because he was working for cash and therefore not paying tax. I think she felt that to ask him his full name would be to imply a criticism, that we were suggesting he should declare the two pounds ten shillings or whatever she paid him to get the hot water back on.

Now I have an IT man called Justin who is handsome and public school-educated and sends me emails with intellectual jokes on the end, and my mother has the Mental Elf.

The Mental Elf sent a man to her house to fetch two dining chairs which my father bought for three shillings each forty years ago, and whose cane seats had been broken for nearly as long. As a concession to bourgeois values, my mother concealed the exploded bits of rush work under cushions, which inevitably meant that when we visited, one of us would sit on them and get stuck. This wasn't in any way amusing. Eventually, she developed a friendship with a woman in the same agoraphobics' group – come to think of it, they were more recovering agoraphobics, since they did manage to get to the group. Anyhow, the other woman got much better and decided to become an occupational therapist and work for the Mental Elf, and so my mother was finally able to get her chairs recaned.

Recently, when the ladies' room was busy in a café, I did what I always do and used the disabled one. I checked there was no wheelchair user desperately rolling towards it with her knees clenched together and went in. There was a thin, red emergency cord, very close to the lavatory itself, and when I was pulling my tights up it got entangled in them. I just managed to separate them before it got pulled and sent a distress signal – to whom? Would everyone in the café hear it? They could hardly have a full-time nurse in Costa Coffee, so presumably it would be some member of staff with two hours' First Aid training who'd come bursting in and witness a disaster, i.e. that my pants didn't match my bra. Except they couldn't, because the door was locked. Is a disabled person in trouble – having a heart attack maybe – supposed to wheel themselves back over to open the door? It would have been a good one for my therapist, if I was still going.

So all I really wanted to say was that's why, when people say therapy has no practical use, I point to those chairs and tell them they're wrong.

10 Hitting the Roof

My mother isn't and never has been Jewish. But I come to suspect she has absorbed some Jewish DNA somewhere along the line, because one weekend I am visiting with Peter and the children and I sit down at the kitchen table.

'Uh-oh, don't sit there,' she says.

'Why? What d'you mean?'

'You'll bump your head.'

I know that I shouldn't get involved in this, should just keep quiet and change seats. But I don't. I say, 'No, I won't. Why?'

'Because you're under the stairs.'

This is, strictly speaking, true. Sticking down from the kitchen ceiling like a kind of large, cube-shaped plaster hernia or a giant's heel is where the stairs turn a corner on their way to the bedrooms. Since the house was built over 300 years ago and then added to piecemeal, it's a fair bet that the original architect didn't envisage it this way. But then he probably didn't envisage the occupants spending a Friday evening telling each other where to sit.

'It's fine. I'm fine.'

'No, would you move? Please.'

'I'm fine. Really.'

'You'll bang your head.'

'No, I *won't*.'

My mother is too anxious to continue the conversation – or her life – because she fears I might hurt my head at an unspecified time in the future.

Now my sister joins in.

'She's right, you know. You should move.'

'Oh, for God's sake.'

Now the two of them are standing on the opposite side of the room staring at me, or rather, at the cuboid bit of ceiling above my head. Even if you had the sort of vision impairment that made you unable to see huge lumps in the ceiling, it's impossible to miss, since my mother has painted a bunch of pink flowers on it to draw people's attention to the danger. And in case *that* doesn't work, she hangs string bags from a nail banged in the side of it, containing bay leaves and the dried husks of what used to be onions. But I am five foot and a bit and in no danger. However fast I stand up I can't hit my head on anything, unless I'm in a Wendy house.

'I've never bumped my head on it the whole time you've lived here. Why would I now?'

'Just sit over here and then you definitely won't,' says my sister, clearly believing I will be reassured by this and not, as in reality, annoyed.

'Look!' I finally yell. 'I'm forty-two! I can decide where to fucking well sit!'

And they both look at me, amazed.

11 Shut Up After the Beep

Recently my mother has started leaving messages on my mobile. She never used to. I've always told her it's so expensive it's only for emergencies, except she doesn't have emergencies. Not for her the plaintive voice on the answerphone whimpering, '*I had a stroke last week but I didn't like to bother you . . .*' No, the only emergency I can imagine for her would be if she ran out of felt tips. And even then she would carry on in pencil.

The other reason I discourage her from calling the mobile is that I don't want her being able to get hold of me just *anywhere*. She isn't someone you can have a brief conversation with; you can't take five minutes to have a quick chat while, say, buying a coffee or waiting for a train. Each call she treats as a kind of sweep of her whole hard disk, a sort of 'Closing Down Sale – Everything Must Be Said!' So they have to be anticipated and prepared for, like holidays. I have to get comfortable, think about where I'm going to sit. If I want to ring her but there's less than half an hour till the next thing I have to do, there's no point, because she won't be able to stop. I say, 'We can talk again, you know. We're not prisoners allowed only one call.' But it makes no difference. Just as 60 per cent of a film's budget these days is the marketing, about 40 per cent of any phone conversation with my mother is me trying to end it. I'd love to have those brief little chats and updates that other people seem to manage, the reports on this and that bit of their life, that add to the great patchwork: Post-it notes, as opposed to entire novels.

Sometimes I'm at a friend's house and their phone rings and they talk for a few minutes then say goodbye, and I say, 'Who was that?'

And they say, 'My mother.'

And I think: how do you do that?

So, because I know we're going to have the long goodbye, I put off ringing her. When we do talk, the end of our calls frequently turn into the exchanges she and my father used to have on the doorstep, when he would be in a hurry and she would think of more and more things she absolutely had to say. And the more she wouldn't let him go, the more impatient he became.

Him: 'I have to go now.'

Her: 'Yes, just one wee thing.'

'I have work.'

'I know, there's just one quick thing.'

'I'M LATE FOR WORK!!'

'You really are a very impatient man.'

And this was after they were divorced.

Now this is her and me on the phone:

Me: 'I have to go now.'

Her: 'Yes, just one more thing.'

'I have to eat/work/go to the loo/make a stable for twenty-five very small horses/scream.'

'Yes, yes, just one wee thing.'

'Look, I have to GO!'

'I have a lot on too, you know!'

And she's right, I am just like my father; she makes me into him.

But don't be misled. She is *not* lonely, *not* bored and *not* looking to me to fill her time. She *has* friends, *has* things in her diary, *is* popular and so on. And I'm honestly not just saying that so you won't hate me. One of the reasons I know, apart from the number of people who call round and phone during our visits, is by the number of Christmas and birth-day cards, the vast majority from people I don't know at all. And sometimes when she's on the phone to me the doorbell goes. It could be a number of things: a neighbour bringing round the parish magazine; someone with some seedlings for the allotment; her friend the retired pharmacist with some new side effects. But though she's on the phone to me, she cannot tell them this. She cannot say, 'Hi, I can't talk now,' in case they get offended.

The revolutionary technology of the cordless phone, which like your neuroses you take with you, proves useless. Convinced that if it's left off the stand for two minutes the battery will run down, she puts it back the second she finishes a conversation. So it is in effect 'cordless' in name only. The base unit is in the kitchen, so that if she happens to be in the sitting room when it rings, she naturally can't get to it in time so the answerphone always comes on. The answerphone is never switched off, and is permanently set to pick up after about one and a half seconds, so every call begins with the screeching of the long beep as she picks it up halfway through your message and you have to say it all again. Which you need to do anyway as she never plays the messages.

If you phone while she's watching TV, she puts the receiver down, in the kitchen of course, and you have to wait while she goes through to the sitting room to turn the TV down. The same applies if, God forbid, the doorbell rings. Down goes the handset on the kitchen counter, and I wait, hearing loud, repeated exchanges booming in the background, until her visitor chooses to slope off. Going to the door *with* the phone, a radical notion I once suggested – thus to convey by visual means the message *I am busy* – is out of the question; the visitor will feel slighted. Similarly, if I'm at her place, and she's on the phone and I have to ask her something – something really quick like, 'Where's the Sellotape?' – she cannot say to the person on the other end, 'Hang on a minute,' and tell me. She has to do frantic semaphoring and mouthing '*I AM ON THE PHONE*' until the other person chooses to end the call or dies. And even then she lowers her head, with the phone right to her ear, until it's almost touching the base unit. This is to make sure no one ever feels, even for a moment, that she is banging down the phone on them.

So, one day she rings my mobile and finds that, unlike with her landline messages, which can go answered for days, I ring her back really quickly.

'Mum, it's me! What is it?'

'I just wanted to say that it would be lovely to see you this weekend and could Peter bring his toolbox?'

'Oh! Right. Great. Only you rang the mobile, so – I thought something had happened.'

'No, no. I'm fine. It's just that when I leave a message on the home phone you never ring me back.'

'I do. Well, OK, sometimes I don't, because you leave such long messages there's nothing to ring you back for. I mean, you say everything in the message. It's like you've said the whole thing.'

'No I don't.'

'You really do.'

I don't know if there's an entry for this in *The Guinness Book of World Records*, but she does leave epic messages. If you think of most messages as haikus, or perhaps verbal emails, hers are Homeric sagas, brimming with colourful description, encompassing references to anything from the changing nature of rural communities to the plots of operas. They could be released on CD.

It surprises me, because she belongs to the generation for whom telephones were luxuries to be used sparingly. A ringing phone was a drama to be regarded with awe, and a long-distance call, i.e. from more than five miles away, an event to be experienced with one's entire family gathered round, preferably standing in their slippers in a draughty hall.

And quite apart from the cost, there was always the possibility that Hitler might be listening. So I'd have thought that anyone born before 1940 would want to get off the line really fast.

Yet the older the person, the longer the message. Shea, my old nanny, leaves warm tributes full of praise for the children, always concluding, 'Love, Shea'. And my friend Jane's mother, also in her eighties, leaves great long messages too, then says at the end, 'By the way, it's Mummy,' in case her daughter doesn't recognize an uninterrupted eight-minute burst of her voice.

My father left very short messages: 'It's your father.'

My mother was the Good One, the non-nuisance who could be relied upon to stay silent for weeks if left undisturbed and who never, ever rang to ask why I hadn't called. Lately, though, this has changed.

I think she just might be starting to feel that time is running out.

12 Power of Attorney

My mother's just got a new PC. This is sensitive territory because she actually got her first computer before I did. Well, an Amstrad. But still, it was a bit embarrassing for me. Your mother isn't supposed to precede you with these things. Varicose veins, or saggy bosoms maybe: not technology. It disturbs the natural order of things. At least she was already living in the country by then, so none of my friends knew. She also recently beat me to an MP3, admittedly because she left it so long to buy her first CD player that now they come with MP3 as standard. Even so, it rankles a bit, particularly as we have still done nothing about getting one ourselves, other than to bash the useless 'Play' button on the ancient Sony in the kitchen and promise the children we will be turning the house into download heaven any minute now, with speakers in every room.

Anyhow, one morning I wake up and remember something important that has to be done, and give my mother a call. I'm hoping it will be a short one, no more than forty minutes.

'Have you got lots on?' she says.

'Yes, you know, the usual. Look,' I say, 'I was talking to Mr Stevens the other day – you know, who sold Dad's house – and he reminded me about the power of attorney.'

'Hm, dear? What about it?'

I can already feel my teeth starting to grind.

'You know! To do it. Get on with it.'

'I'm not quite – what do you mean?'

'Oh, come on, Mother! For God's sake, you must remember talking about it. It was your idea!'

'Was it?'

'Oh *God* . . . !'

Shit, it's already too late. The thing about power of attorney is, by the time you need it, you can no longer legally apply. It's like a vaccination: you have to have it *before* your neural pathways turn to semolina.

'Pow-er of attor-ney! You know. In case you lose your marbles.'

She doesn't mind my saying these things. She's not bothered by death or senility or incontinence or any of the nightmares associated with ageing of

118

which I am petrified. She is even capable of finding them funny.

There is a pause. Is she still on the end of the line, or has she died? At least that would save us the hassle.

'For God's sake!' I snap. 'You were the one who suggested it! Don't you remember *anything*?'

'But we have.'

'Have what? What d'you mean?'

'Done the power of attorney.'

This brings home to me, somewhat graphically, why we need it, though I must say I am shocked by her total blankness.

'Of course we haven't done it! I'd remember, because I'd *have signed it*.'

This really is beyond even a normal person's patience. Another pause.

'You did sign it.'

I think. I search my memory: nothing.

'Of course I didn't.'

'No, really.'

'But—'

'Don't you remember, dear? You came here with Mr Gorringe. It was witnessed by Joan. You brought a cake.'

119

I run another check: still nothing. No documents, no Mr Gorringe, no Joan, no cake, no nothing.

'Who's Mr Gorringe?'

'My solicitor. They have the office in Ashford with the gargoyle on the top that when you were a little girl you—'

'Do they? Does he? Right. Well. Good. That's OK then.'

I sigh heavily. This is just the latest in a series of memory-related disasters. It wouldn't be so bad if I didn't have a mother who can quote poetry she read sixty years ago.

'You've just got a lot on your mind, with the kids and all.'

'That's no excuse. Anyhow, I don't want to just remember which day they both have swimming or a cake sale or Ancient Roman Day, and the name of the school newt. And not – the heroine of *Middlemarch*.'

'You've just got different priorities,' she says.

'Yeah? Well, I don't *want* those priorities. It's like my brain's a shelf: one thing comes on, another falls off. And a bloody small shelf, as well. I read that book on my honeymoon!'

'It's partly the stage they're at: there's a lot to

remember. I bet you don't forget to collect them from school, do you?'

'No. But I really am losing it on other fronts. You know how I used to be able to remember phone numbers? And addresses: I could look at an address once and know where I was going. Now I end up in the car with Peter, saying, "It's on the left" when it isn't, or "It's number 83" when it's actually 47, or forgetting it completely.'

'I'm sure it's not that bad.'

She has no idea.

A few months ago we walked up and down Brompton Road and *Old* Brompton Road because I couldn't remember which one of them contained my favourite French restaurant. Twice. Then, just as I was about to buy a new winter coat, I found the perfectly good one I bought last year, of which I had no memory.

And in the summer holidays about three years back, we booked a B&B in Hampshire and halfway down the M3 I realized I'd left all the details at home.

'I couldn't remember the name of the house, or their names, or the village or anything.'

'Gosh!' she says. 'What did you do?'

'I rang someone at school who had the list of class phone numbers to get the number of the woman who'd recommended it, who luckily was at home, and got the name and number from her.'

'So you got there in the end? Well done.'

'But it was so embarrassing, having to admit I'd set off without it. I could hear this sort of gasp of incredulity down the phone.'

'Oh well, you can't get through life without ever being embarrassed.'

'In the past I would have had it all in my head. What kind of cake did I bring anyway? Was it a home-made one?'

'When?'

'When we did the power of attorney.'

'Well, it was a few years ago. I'm not sure. I think so. Orange, would it have been?'

'Probably. D'you think I should try and have a test or something? What am I going to do?'

'I honestly think you just have a lot on your plate. Actually, if you don't mind, I've got to ring off. I'm being taken out for a meal this evening.'

'Of course. Have a lovely time. Who by?'

'Bill the retired pharmacist, and the Major and his wife.'

'Lovely.'

Normally I queue up for snippets from Bill the retired pharmacist and his trusty copy of the *British National Formulary*, which, in a village populated by variously medicated seniors, makes him extremely sought after. But right now, I've lost the urge.

And my mother, who in three years will be eighty, says, 'Look after your wee self. Bye just now,' her voice dropping softly as she never likes to deliver an abrupt farewell.

About a year later I bump into one of our neighbours.

'How are you?' I say.

'Not too good. Well, it's my mum. She's got vascular dementia.'

'Oh no. How awful. When did this happen?'

'Well, we first noticed it around Christmas. We talked about it. D'you remember?'

'Um . . .'

We stand there, looking at each other.

'Shit, looks like I've got it too,' I say, and we laugh.

My mother may have got a computer and an MP3 before me, but clearly I'll be the first one into the Twilight Home for the Pedantically Bewildered. And the thing that frightens me even more is wondering what I'll do when she's no longer able to visit.

13 Better or Worse: Mum into Granny

When I was pregnant for the first time, I asked Judith, my Alexander teacher, 'When you become a mother, does your relationship with your own mother get better or worse?'

And she thought for a moment and said, 'Both.'

My mother can't come to see us because she has tingly feet. I wonder at first if it's a severe case of *avoidancis familitis*, as the first I hear of this incapacity is the week of the children's Sports Day, when she can't make the ninety-minute train journey to us but appears at my sister's, a whole hour further away, the same day. The children, aged only three and four, don't notice. But I look at the other grandparents there and, to my surprise, feel a kind of ache.

My mother greeted the news of her impending

new status with just the pleasure and pride I had hoped for. Peter and I went down to tell her we were going to have a baby, champagne was opened, everybody kissed everybody and I thought we were entering a new, happy phase.

Within a few weeks, however, she complained that I wasn't keeping her up to date with the pregnancy.

'You never tell me what's going on,' she said.

'That's probably because there isn't anything going on,' I said. 'I feel fine.'

In the absence of anything more concrete, and knowing her fondness for medical detail, I sent her a copy of the scan report.

'Fascinating, don't you think?'

'It's very kind of you, dear,' she said. 'But all those graphs and figures just make you more anxious, don't they?'

'No,' I said. 'The opposite. They show there's nothing wrong.'

This did not sound like her at all. Information make you anxious? Knowledge is power; we both knew that.

My approach to health and sickness was inspired entirely by her. At school, seeing friends kept off with mere coughs or snuffles, I treasured my superior knowledge, as I bent over my maths or geography, that they were not really ill at all! Not for us wasted afternoons at home, or pointless trips to the doctor to demand antibiotics for viruses they could not treat.

Given a set of typical symptoms my mother could usually come up with a diagnosis. It was she who taught me, having answered late-night calls when she lived with a doctor, that 95 per cent of all abdominal pains are wind. (If woken in the night by belly cramps, you should get on the floor on all fours, to allow the trapped air to move along to the end.) My relatively sober approach to aches, pains and infant symptoms, which has proved so reassuring since becoming a parent, is thanks to her. Yet, rather than bringing us closer, the scan report seemed to come between us.

It may have been the conjunction of technology with motherhood. She worked for the NCT in its early days, when it campaigned to win more control for women at a time when the advice of most obstetricians was 'Lie back and shut up'. So, given that she may well have been nursing a vision of the arrival of her first grandchild delivered painlessly in a birthing pool with Bach playing in the background and not a heart monitor or epidural in sight, my keenness on technology must have been a bit disheartening.

Then I really feared I had blown it when I revealed my intention to have an elective Caesarean – something I had avoided telling her for months. But she put aside her ideals and embraced the decision simply because it was the one I had made.

'I will support you fully,' she said, as deep an expression of unconditional approval as I have ever received from her. But the moment of closeness evaporated, as such moments have always done with us, and we reverted once again to our habitual precarious position.

Fourteen months after Lawrence, we had a girl, Lydia. I might not be much of a daughter, I thought, but look! I had produced these two wonders of nature: fair-haired, peach-skinned and, by three, able to charm the pants off anyone with their chat. Lydia even looked like her. She would adore them unreservedly and greet their every tiny step towards maturity with wonder and delight. Given time, they might even heal whatever was wrong between us.

She swung into the procurement side with enthusiasm, sourcing essential bits of kit – and two of everything – so we could visit her without having to put up and dismantle cots. But the great new connection I hoped for, the whole extra dimension it would bring to all our lives, didn't materialize in the way I had imagined.

Invited to play with them, she read the paper. Left in charge to give them supper she didn't feed them but left the food on the table and declared them to be poor eaters. She had told me wonderful bedtime stories, often of her own invention, but never read to them. One night I took the initiative and told them Granny would come up and read them a story. She stiffly refused. I put off reaching the inevitable conclusion, that her new role bored her. Despite having friends who embraced grand-parenthood without becoming mere understudies for the children's parents, she appeared to regard it as less a reward of later life than a second-best hobby for people with nothing more exciting to do.

Still, she was the only grandparent they had. And even when I felt like witholding my treasures from her, I still brought them, sometimes remaining in the hall for as long as possible before coming in, like my father on Friday evenings in the early months when the separation was still raw.

I also realized that conflicts could be defused or even escaped altogether by the need to leave the room for babywipes or changes of clothes. And with the children as buffer, I felt I could take an emotional step back, even use them as a shield to deflect the negative energy that crackled between us.

But then, when Lawrence started to string words together, they began to have little conversations and she began to talk to him, about the colour of his socks or the tractor up the road. She gave him her shepherd's pie – 'made with real shepherds' – which he wolfed down appreciatively, and took him to her allotment, where he suddenly developed an interest in fruit and vegetables. It helped my frame of mind no end that while they were out I got to read a whole Sunday paper. She drew him a book of big and small tractors, and immortalized their visits with another book, a fantasy in which everything he went to pick for Granny – beans, raspberries, potatoes – turned out to be made of chocolate. And though in the story Granny did not at first believe it, in *The Chocolate Allotment* the impossible really did come true.

Then, when they were about five and six, Peter and I got her to babysit by default.

'Just nipping out for a bit!' we called, and went to the pub.

We giggled guiltily over our pints like truants, but it helped by making space for a more active relationship between them. With us out of the way for a while she could experience them on her terms. And sure enough, when we returned she was dispensing fascinating nuggets about birds and insects and communicating the way she felt happiest, through drawing. The children were absolutely rapt, and as we stood in the doorway watching them, I felt that a big corner had been turned. From now on, things would be different.

14 Grow Your Own Memories

One of my favourite weekend activities is to sit in the house, on a sunny day, reading the gardening sections of the papers, so I can cut out and save articles about growing your own vegetables. Along with ordering a luscious-looking catalogue from Seeds of Italy to adorn the kitchen counter, this is the closest I have ever come to actually growing anything you can eat.

So I was, to put it mildly, both impressed and envious when my mother first rang up to invite us to her new allotment.

'It's just a half-allotment, actually,' she said modestly. 'I'm sharing it with my friend Maureen.'

I felt excited and somewhat pathetic. At seventy-four she was about to embark on an entirely new activity and one that required considerable stamina. Apart from going into the garden each summer to pull up a few weeds, I am, as I say, basically an armchair gardener. Once a year I get up early to go to the cheap flower market and buy a carful of plants, most of which are unsuitable for the type of conditions we have, or the north-facing garden, or soil which is so clay-like you could use it to make pots. So by autumn almost everything has died, a fact which we manage to avoid dealing with by not going out there at all between October and March. And when spring arrives, we're not much better. The most strenuous thing I've done lately has been to go up a stepladder to prune the bay tree and that was only because, if I didn't, Peter was going to go out there and 'tidy it up a bit', i.e. hack it to death.

And instead of coming round and saying, as I would, 'No wonder everything dies; you've got all the wrong plants,' or 'Why don't you play to your strengths and just have a patio?' my mother has offered on all her visits to walk round and make helpful notes. And even when, on each successive visit, she can see that we've forgotten the notes, or misinterpreted them, or just lost them altogether, she says patiently, 'Well, a garden does evolve. It can't all happen overnight.'

Clearly, gardening brings out the best in both of us. So an allotment boded well. For her there was the added satisfaction of being able to provide her grandchildren with the same seed-to-table experience she had as a child, when her father and uncle grew peas and beans, though with the difference that Lawrence and Lydia would be allowed to play among the runner-bean canes and pick whatever they liked, as opposed to being told to keep off in case they accidentally broke off a leaf.

'I'm really doing it for them,' she said.

'So what are you going to grow?'

'Chard.'

'Right. Which is . . .'

'It's like spinach. It's full of nutrients and absolutely delicious.'

'I'm not sure the children will really go for that. Anything else?'

'Jerusalem artichokes. Also delicious.'

'Urgh . . . Are you going to grow anything normal?'

'Of course I am, you silly girl.'

'Such as?'

'Runner beans.'

'Well, *we* love them. The children don't. Yet.'

'Well, if they don't eat vegetables . . .'

'They do "eat vegetables", just not those ones.'

'Really? Which?'

'Oh, for God's sake. Carrots. Broccoli.'

'Well, maybe they can learn.'

'You could try growing stuff they actually want to eat.'

'I am doing. There'll be leeks. And potatoes.'

'Great. We love those.'

'And Maureen's going to do raspberries.'

'Raspberries! Our favourite!'

'Well, we'll be sharing everything, so they can have some of those too.'

We went down to help. For Peter and me, desk-bound townies, the chance to reap the physical and spiritual satisfaction of manual labour was a revel-ation. Well, less of a revelation to him, since he did once work in a pea-processing plant and at least knew how to hold a spade. I was astonished by how tiring it was, so he and Mum did almost all the dig-ging and planting, while I weeded for a few minutes at a time before stopping to draw a weary, non-calloused hand across my brow like a character from Chekhov but holding a beer, sort of Masha meets Homer Simpson. After learning that the raspberries weren't going to ripen for another three months, the children somewhat lost interest. Lawrence did about three minutes' digging, then ran off to visit the people with the exotic birds in their garden and to play on the abandoned tractor. And apart from fighting him for a go on that, Lydia did almost nothing at all. So my mother's dream, of three generations digging happily together, did not quite come to fruition.

We had to wait until July for our first sight of them eating the raspberries straight off the bushes, but it was worth it. When I weeded the new strawberry patch, picked a lettuce and leaned against the toolshed, admiring my dirty hands, it seemed that for a moment, all our worries had gone with the sun beyond the runner-bean canes and everyone's expectations had been met.

I was jolted from my short-lived reverie by Lawrence, who wanted to know when we were going to the pub.

'You said we could have lemonade.'

'Sssh! In a minute.'

My mother raised a critical eyebrow, but the spell had not been broken, quite.

We hadn't finished and I didn't want her to think I was 'giving in'.

But soon we picked up our tools and strolled to our reward, seeming at last truly like members of the same tribe, the sun obligingly backlighting the children, whose raspberry-stained fingers were still pink the next day: a perfect, rosy memory to take home.

15 You Don't Know How Lucky You Are 1: 22 Things My Mother Has Never Said

(1) Any chance of a cup of tea? If it's not *too* much trouble.

(2) Why are you always offering me tea all the time? You know I'll be up all night.

(3) You're in and out of that hospital every other day. Don't you think those poor nurses have enough to do? Anyhow, what do you want with all these scans? It's just one more thing to worry about. In our day we had to make do with a midwife listening to your tummy with a glass. And midwives were only for the rich. My mother grew up in the tenements and they only had the rag-and-bone woman. *Her* mother gave birth in the cotton mill, and the baby choked to death on all that fluff. She wasn't allowed time

off for the funeral either. She had to stay at her loom or be docked a year's pay. But she knew her place.

(4) If the doctor says you need a scan, don't you think he knows what he's talking about?

(5) You want to get away from that computer for a change. The Interweb may be all very clever but it can't mop a fevered baby's brow, can it? It can't purse its lips and tell you to pull your socks up. It can't run an empire either. In my day we had something called common sense. But of course it's all out of fashion now.

(6) That child should be playing outside. It's not snowing *that* hard.

(7) What's that child doing playing outside? She'll catch her death.

(8) What's this Calpol you keep giving them? What's wrong with good old-fashioned gripe water, I'd like to know? There's nothing wrong with that child a thimbleful of gin and a slap on the legs wouldn't cure.

(9) All that child needs is a cuddle from his mother, not a Ninjatendo box.

(10) What that child needs is to get away from the television and read a book for a change.

(11) She's got her head in a book all the time. What that child needs is to get outside in the fresh air.

(12) Homoeopathy??? All those free doctors and you go giving them *water*. Which you spend good money on. When the NHS came in we all lined up for free teeth. It was like Christmas. And here you are giving them 'rescue remedy'. My father had his legs blown off in the Somme. I'd like to see you give him 'rescue remedy'. Your grandmother would be turning in her grave – if she still had one. She was dug up and moved to Croydon to make way for a Tesco's. But that's progress for you. People these days would rather have multipacks of croissants than show respect for the dead.

(13) It's not good for them, being driven everywhere all the time. They've got legs, haven't they? My uncle was crippled by a runaway brewer's dray. He would have given his right leg to be able to walk ten miles to school in the rain.

(14) What you're doing going on a 'walking holiday' I don't know. You've got a perfectly good car sitting on the drive. My mother had to carry forty-eight pounds of shopping twelve miles up the hill every day. She'd be turning in her grave to see that car going to waste.

(15) What, off out again? To 'work'? If you spent more time on your children and – yes, I *do* say so, young lady, less time on your *career* . . . Well, I'm only saying what everyone else is thinking. Your husband's got a job, hasn't he? You're making it look as though he can't provide. In my day we'd have been glad to be at home. We didn't have all this 'choice' they go on about. I spent my menopause down the mine, not sitting about in some 'meeting'.

(16) 'Childcare'? I've never heard of such a thing. My mother brought up twelve children without any help. And she only lost two up the chimney and one to scarlet fever. People need 'help' these days to cross the road. It's ridiculous.

(17) You're not too old to be put over my knee and spanked, you know.

(18) How can they appreciate anything with all these toys? We made do with a pin and an old cotton reel. And the pin was bent. And we didn't complain and beg for a My Mini Pony all the time. I had one doll to last me through two world wars. And I got blood poisoning from the lead paint. It was all part of a normal childhood, along with whooping cough, polio and seeing Mr Townley from the allotments exposing himself.

(19) Don't you ever turn that thing off? We made our own entertainment. Singing round the kettle. And when the V1s came down we stood round the hole where the kettle used to be and sang round that. We knitted 400 balaclavas on one night in the Anderson shelter alone. When my mother was killed by shrapnel she never dropped a stitch.

(20) You've got 4,800 channels and you hardly watch it. My mother would have killed to be able to shop on the television. She had to walk twenty miles for a pint of milk, not get it on the Interweb. And the butcher was on the other side of the Pennines. We had to set off in October to get our slice of bacon for Christmas.

(21) 'Bonding'? Ten minutes after giving birth to you I was at the hairdresser's having my hair clapped in irons. And I was back at the stove to have your father's tea ready, not lounging on the settee 'bonding'. And I never greeted him at the door in 'leggings'. I stood to attention with my lipstick on and my corset pressed, not looking like I'd been dragged through a hedge backwards. If we'd had a hedge, which we didn't. Hedges were only for the well-to-do, and quite right too.

(22) You don't appreciate the luxuries you have nowadays. Shower gel? We had one bar of soap to go round the whole village. It was our turn to use it on the third Wednesday in the month. My mother's family used to come all the way from Burnley. Shampoo and conditioner? We washed our hair in Guinness – and only after father had drunk it or we'd get a strap to the backside. Velcro? We had to tie our husbands on with string. Flavoured condoms? We had to keep the bedroom door shut. Ensuite bidets? We got our first toilet in 1968. It was in the town hall and we had to wait our turn like everyone else. My father didn't move his bowels

in the indoors until 1981. Deodorant? My mother didn't sit around perfuming her armpits; she was too busy being captured by the Japanese. Post-natal depression? We didn't have time to sit around being depressed; we were too busy blocking the toilets with self-administered abortions. Post-traumatic stress disorder? Mrs Kowslowski on the corner was raped by the Russians and never had post-traumatic stress disorder. She screamed non-stop from 1942 to the Queen's Golden Jubilee and never complained once. My mother had fourteen miscarriages and never complained about post-traumatic stress. She was dead at twenty-one and glad to be.

16 Getting Out the Knives

This is to be, though I don't know it yet, one of her last visits to us. I collect her from the station, drive her back to our place, let her in and go out to get something from the car. When I come back in she's standing in the middle of the kitchen, in her coat, with her bag over her shoulder.

'Mum, what is it?'

'You don't seem to have any heating.'

'Are you cold?'

'Obviously that's what I'm saying!'

'Well, why don't you just ask me to put it on?'

'I am asking, you silly girl!'

'No, you are NOT. Asking is when you bloody well ASK!'

She didn't used to do this. It's only been over the four years or so that we've been in this house. Each time she's done the same thing: stood in the middle of the room as if waiting for something. And each time it's turned out that she *is* waiting for something, like food or a cup of tea or to be warmer, but hasn't asked.

My father once drew a cartoon of a man asking a woman, 'What do you want?'

And the woman is saying, 'I want you to know without my telling you.'

Once, in the middle of tea, she got up and started going round the room feeling the radiators.

'What are you DOING?' I barked.

Not only was I profoundly irritated, there were other people there and it looked weird.

'You don't seem to have any heating in this house.'

'Are – you – *COLD*?'

'Well, ha-ha, of course!'

'Well, fucking well say so then! Say, "Please can you put the heating on!" What the fuck's wrong with you?'

The other guests gazed down into their cups.

I go upstairs to the loo and when I come back she's opening all the drawers.

'Are you looking for something?'

'This appears to be a house without cutlery.'

'What do you mean? Of course we have cutlery! I'll get it. What do you want, anyway?'

'Well, a knife would be nice.'

I pull open the drawer in a temper and bang it shut. She falls back, clutching her hand to her chest.

'Oh! Oh! What was that?'

'It's a *drawer*! What do you want a knife for, anyway? Can I please do it, whatever it is?'

'No, thank you. I'm just making myself a sandwich.'

When in my own house I like to make the food and serve it. Having friends round – giving them drinks, food, anything – is my favourite activity. Ironically, I may well have learned this from her. When I was growing up, our flat had only a cramped kitchen-diner, yet any visitor – friend, colleague or gasman – would be invited to eat, or at the very least to sit down and relate their life story over a cup of tea. It explained why things didn't get fixed very easily, with plumbers and handymen drawn into conversation, their original purpose forgotten. Now, the woman from whom I learned the joys of hospitality wanders round my kitchen, serving herself as if in a hostel, an impression reinforced by the fact that she is still in her coat. I give her the knife, and with surprising swiftness, she gets breadcrumbs, butter and bits of cheese – I have a slight cheese phobia – all over every surface. I wipe up, vigorously, and open the china cupboard.

'At least have it on a *plate*.'

As part of her rebellion against the forces of petit bourgeoisness, she often puts food straight on to the table. I grab the sandwich, put it on the plate and march her over to a chair.

'You're evidently not making an evening meal then?'

'What? When? Of course I am. It's called supper.'

'Well, I don't see any sign of it.'

'That's because it's four o'clock.'

'Oh. Well, I missed lunch actually, if you want to know.'

'How would I *know* that? ASK! For fuck's sake, can't you just be *normal*?'

But she doesn't want to be normal: normal is boring. If she did something normal she might become ordinary.

'I didn't want to bother you,' she adds, as she sits down on a pile of newspapers. 'You're always so *busy*.'

This is a reference to my habit of tidying up, putting the papers into a pile and so on, while she is in the room. It keeps some air between us and helps diffuse the intensity of what my father used to call 'all that relating'. If I sit down first, she sits way too close, sometimes even landing partly on top of me.

Or she sits down in the middle of the sofa, leaving half a space, a sort of size 8 space, on each side. My way round this is to perch on the arm, sit on the coffee table or not sit down at all. Hence I am always 'busy'.

There's another reason. I want to be able to retreat quickly if she drops one of her barbs into the conversation, little darts that shoot across, usually when other people aren't within earshot, and embed themselves under my skin.

'I'm clearly not getting any grandchildren' was from when I was considering motherhood despite questionable ovaries, and 'you fucking yuppie' when I told her I was replacing our old – uncomfortable – family chairs. This one was at least funny. Or she'll choose a serial killer from the news and talk about him determinedly, dismissing my protests. If the children are there, my protectiveness is treated as oppression: she, the Voice of Freedom, must bravely speak out! The personal darts last the longest. The more I try to pull them out, the deeper they go, until I am charging around like a bull while she, the matador, flourishes her cloak to the roar of her internal crowd.

When I lose my temper she says, 'You're just like your father,' and she is right.

I used to feel ashamed when she said this. Then I noticed that when I didn't rise to the bait – which was not very often – she got angry instead.

At supper, I try unsuccessfully to douse her with alcohol but only end up drinking her seconds as well as mine. Afterwards I lie in bed, trying to read a book while my eyes slither across the page.

'Have you tried deciding not to mind?' says Peter, his voice butting into the silence like an ad for a product I don't want.

'Christ! Not this again!'

He is convinced I will take this advice any day now; all he has to do is keep on giving it.

'I do mind! Anyway, she wants me to lose it, you can tell.'

'Well, it's no fun for the rest of us.'

'I just want her to be *normal*.'

'Well, she isn't. She's unusual. You've got to try and appreciate her the way she is.'

'Why? She doesn't appreciate me the way I am.'

'If you don't watch out, she'll die and you'll be trapped in guilt and unexpressed remorse.'

'He says supportively. Gee, thanks.'

'I'm just saying.'

'Well, try *not* saying. Try shutting the fuck up about a relationship you're not in.'

'Yes, I know, I'm just saying you don't want to be stuck in this position of anger your whole life.'

'Yeah, well, what happened to your strategy of always looking on the bright side?'

He pauses for a moment then puts on his I'm-going-to-be-helpful-but-only-from-a-position-of-superiority face. And I know he is going to tell me something he has told me loads of times before.

'I remember when I wasn't getting on with my father, going to see this guy on this job I was doing. And it was going really badly. And he said—'

'The guy who said apologize to your father: I remember.'

'What he actually said was, "Until you make peace with your father and stepmother you won't be able to fulfil your potential."'

'Whatever. You told me.'

My husband's theory of psychology is of the blinding revelation from a wise man followed by a turning point. He must have told me this about a hundred times.

'You were thirty.'

'Twenty.'

'Whatever. It doesn't apply to me.'

'Well, OK. What if your father had died before you made it up?'

'We'll never know. I was lucky.'

'She's going to die and you've never said, "I love you."'

'Are you still here? How do you know I've never said it? Who are you, Trisha? For God's sake!'

'I'm just so glad I thanked my father for sending me to a school I loved before he died.'

'Well, bully for you. Now bugger off.'

Along with the blinding revelation and the magic turning point, he also loves the deathbed reconciliation. I'm thinking he should just go and write for *Casualty* and leave me the hell alone.

Every time he brings this stuff up it's not only that he seems to think I've never heard it before, it's as if I don't know the benefit, that I *want* it all to end with a lot of bad feeling and guilt. I swear he's treating this whole issue exactly the same as when we had to have the back of the house painted. He explained it was because the rain was getting in and would have eventually buggered the window frames, whereas I would have spent the money on a bigger TV. I think he believes you can prevent guilt the same way.

And underlying it all is the sheer absurdity of getting advice on emotional conflict from someone who's never been even slightly self-destructive or depressed. It's like a size 8 woman leaning over the buffet at a party as you pile your plate up, and asking if you've ever tried Diet Coke. Well, let me tell you this: I've been battling with this half my life.

'I was on the couch when you were still playing with Meccano,' I tell him. And, when that doesn't work, 'Just – shut up.'

We go to sleep without resolving anything.

In the morning, before he drives her to the station, my mother says, 'I don't want to come here any more.'

And I say, 'Fine.'

And I close the door and go back to my life.

17 Help Is a Four-letter Word

Here's a jolly thing about growing up they don't tell you. Just when you think you've got your life sorted, your parents start falling to bits.

'When your mother gets older, you start to become the parent,' says my friend Mark, who stands back and sees the patterns in life.

'You mean I get to sweep in and take charge? Er, no . . .'

Parents get to tell people what to do. Or they used to. I mean, it's an imperfect world and we live in child-centred times, but we do, at least some of the time, get to be the boss. I read an article somewhere pointing out that when our generation were kids we did what our parents wanted, and then we became parents and now do what our children want. When are we going to get our turn? But there's a final stage of frustration and disempowerment and it's by far the worst of the three.

With my mother I have no authority at all.

She likes things the way they are; I want them cleaner, neater. She won't put on a clean shirt, doesn't want a purse that closes without the aid of a rubber band, doesn't want a cup of tea in bed in the mornings made by the electric teapot. She switches the lights off; I put them on. She unplugs the TV and all the lamps; I plug them back in. She piles her papers on the table we're going to have supper on; I take them off. She lays the table with big, earthenware plates; I swap them for the china ones.

I bark, 'Your purse is by the door where anyone can grab it and your bank statements are all over the stairs!'

'It's fine.'

She doesn't have a great deal for anyone to steal, but the exposure of her private affairs upsets me as much as if her skirt were tucked into her tights.

'You really don't want just anyone being able to see these. I mean, you really don't.'

She looks at me levelly and says, 'They're fine.'

So no one's the parent: we're both teenagers.

The post-feminist irony of this hasn't escaped me, when I go down to her place and plead with her to let me clean up. Me, whose husband says I could do with a touch of obsessive-compulsive disorder. So I resort to doing things she can't prevent – may, just possibly, even welcome – like getting shopping and changing bulbs. But I ache to bring harmony to this giant nest of papers, like a multi-storey hamster cage, and long to clear a path through the years of accumulated clutter. She defends her homeland fiercely, the Yanomami tribeswoman fending off loggers. Oh, please let me clean, I say: *please*. I put on the TV for distraction while, ever so discreetly, I bend down and wipe inside the fridge. You remember the magic compass in *Pirates of the Caribbean* that shows you your heart's desire? When I get it off Jack Sparrow – *Captain* Jack Sparrow – it will point to a bottle of Cif.

It's not that I want to boss her around, fun though that sounds; I just want to be able to fix – something. Anything. To be able to come away from there having had an effect. Instead I feel I am sucked back into chaos. Even for a weekend, it feels both uncontained *and* engulfing, like being on the edge of a cliff with a duvet over my face. I feel the papers, broken lamps, smelly cloths and pointless household catalogues – all the *stuff* – is going to rise up and suffocate me and I won't be able to get out. And of course it never actually quite does. It's like those scenes from *Thunderbirds* and old TV thrillers. The level of the water in the room where the heroes are tied up is always just above their chins. And when they cut away and cut back, the fuse burning along so furiously is still always just about to reach the bomb, the timer still shows 0.07 seconds till the end of the world and so on. That's how I feel in this house.

But to what end am I trying to inflict this 'help'? It means something different to each of us. In old films, whenever a baby is about to be born the doctor rushes in and says, 'Bring lots of hot water and towels!' And the inhabitants dash out and return with what looks like the contents of the bathroom department of John Lewis. But to *help*, to actually improve the baby's and the mother's chances of not bleeding to death, what they *should* be bringing is pain relief, a foetal heart monitor and a way to measure her blood pressure. But the doctor never rushes in and says, 'Quick, someone! Go out and invent the epidural!'

Or a real example: films and television thrillers always show cars bursting into flames after they crash, and the people being dragged out at the last minute, two seconds before the wreck goes up in a fireball. Always. But in real life cars very rarely catch fire. When Peter and I were in a car accident, and four of us lay in the wreckage in various states of injury, none of the people who stopped pulled us out. And this was good, because, though it would probably have been OK for the others, I was upside down with my head jammed right over on to one shoulder. So if I had been pulled out the wrong way, I might well have ended up with irreparably damaged cervical vertebrae. In other words, those kind fellow motorists might have 'helped' by breaking my neck.

The stranger who told me to support my baby's head, the first time I ever took Lawrence into town, probably thought she was helping too. But considering that he was lying down safely on a big padded seat in a café as opposed to hanging out of his sling on a precipice, she didn't actually need to intervene. Help is a rather subjective concept. In fact, I'd say that a lot of people who see themselves as massively into helping are in fact massively into sticking their noses in. And I should know: I'm one of them.

In town, for instance, the minute I see someone looking a bit lost, or even *thinking* about getting a map out, I want to rush up and give them directions. I'm just dying for them to ask me where the Tate is, or the London Eye. Or even better, where to eat.

Two Canadians stopped me near where we live a few months back and asked if there was a Starbucks nearby. Well, I couldn't just say no. I couldn't even just say no and curse the mention of the name. Oh no, I had to explain why we would *never* want a branch of that hideous chain in our area, why our own local coffee shops were so much nicer, full of integrity and had better service, and where exactly they could be found. The Canadians wanted a cup of coffee; what they got was a review of the pros and cons of the cafés of south London and a dissertation on the oppression of Ethiopian coffee farmers by World Trade Organization price fixing. They eventually got away from me and fled – probably to the nearest McDonald's.

When friends tell me their troubles I'm even worse. I don't just want to do what friends are meant to do, i.e. listen. I want to give them advice, and for them to take it. And having done that, for them to come back to me next time and tell me their lives are now fixed. It's not even just the ego trip; I really do want to see their problems solved. It's like a slightly complicated version of people who can't go to sleep if their clothes aren't put away. I can't relax if someone I know wants to find a boyfriend or change their job. If they'd just do what I say I could stop worrying about them. I can't accept that any solution is in their hands, not mine.

This is why proper therapists don't tell you to leave your job/have that affair/get divorced, because that would be furthering their agenda, not yours. They may *seem* as if they do, but their role is to help you get closer to what you want, not what they think you should. It's why nurses are the most amazing people, because they genuinely help those in need, without following them home from hospital – as I probably would – demanding that they stick to their exercises and eat properly and take their pills. Maybe it's because when I was very young I wanted my parents to stop being unhappy so I could relax and enjoy my life. Or maybe it has nothing to do with that and I'm just a controlling, nosy old bag.

Either way, it's a major reason I find family life so challenging. As parents we're supposed to nurture our children but let them grow up and evolve their own ways of solving problems, blah blah blah. And we're also meant to give them the basic tools to develop those skills. But what exactly is the right way to do it? When does merely giving them the skills turn into doing it for them? It sounds so obvious, yet each of us draws the line in a different place.

When I was young, children were less pampered and had far more autonomy. And I'm not talking about making dens on bomb sites and a cuff round the ear from the local bobby; I mean in the relatively recent 1970s. At age eleven, I did the washing up and even some ironing, and went to school across London on the bus. My sister and I were left alone now and then when my mother went out. This week Lawrence had a friend to tea – a ten-year-old – and when he asked for a drink I invited him to get up, get a glass and fill it from the tap.

'There are clean glasses in there,' I said, and watched, amazed, as he waited by the dishwasher.

'I don't know how to open it,' he said.

This kid is a star pupil and I'm sure his mother is a paragon of helpfulness, but I don't fancy Lydia's being his girlfriend in ten years.

And so we get back to my mother. My idea of 'helping' is to clean, tidy, beat back the chaos. Hers is for me *not* to.

The irony here, and it's one that Peter *never* tires of pointing out, is that at home I'm nothing like this. I'm quite happy to sit in my own house, glass of wine in hand, with the mess building up around me. I can drift through the day and on into the evening, and at weekends quite possibly in my nightie, like a character in a Tennessee Williams play. While he eats his single apple for breakfast and leaps around the room, cleaning and tidying and sorting, I lounge at the counter in my dressing gown, working my way through eggs, bacon and toast, surrounded by half-opened bills and letters and sections of about-to-be-read newspaper.

Once at my mother's, however, I turn into one of those busy, bustling women who can't sit down for a minute because they always have to be wiping, or sorting, or polishing, or bobbing to the sink to wash up their own cup. The ones who, if you invite them to dinner, refuse to sit down and be a guest, but have to come into the kitchen and *do* something. We had one round here once who, ignoring my polite refusals, marched straight past me, took hold of one of my saucepans and started stirring. I had to lead her away and block her in with some sofa cushions. Those women radiate nervous, targetless energy. They're among the people I find most irritating, and yet when I'm at my mother's I become one of them.

It's not just that I have this extreme 'helping' side lurking within me – though largely dormant at home, as Peter would like noted . . . yes, all right, I've said that now. The environment she lives in brings out my anal-retentiveness so dramatically that, having been living secretly inside me, it suddenly bursts out like Alien and – as far as she's concerned – sets about destroying the whole ship. I seem compelled to do it, because otherwise it's as if by letting the mess swirl around me I'm endorsing it. I'm so keen not to espouse her New-Agey, 'chaos is creative' bollocks that I have to stand up and denounce it. Also, I do have this tiny contrariness issue.

Do you, when you find yourself in the company of someone who announces that 'all consumerism is evil' or something, think their certainty is so annoying that, when you open your mouth to answer, you come off sounding like Rupert Murdoch? Then at a party you fall into conversation with a banker and hear yourself calling for the nation's shopping centres to be turned into collective farms. Or maybe that's just me.

Recently I met up with an old friend who went to one of those ladylike schools where you don't actually learn anything. She's a lovely woman, but immediately I became irritated by her almost wilful ignorance of the world.

'And how was that great holiday you had?' she asked. 'In Trini-what's-it.'

'You mean Trinidad,' I said, somewhat briskly. 'Except we went to Tobago. It's the much smaller—'

'That's it,' she said. 'Where they do that tinkling on the dustbin lids.'

She meant steel band music.

I had to get out of there before I turned into Jeremy Paxman.

Then, also recently, I met a Real Journalist, who'd lived in Moscow and lots of other quite challenging places, and suddenly, from being a reasonably articulate, not entirely stupid individual, I turned into this: 'I heard a piece on the radio, about one of those countries that used to be in the Soviet Union. Er . . .'

'Uzbekistan?' he said helpfully.

'No, that wasn't it. It's run by a chap who named the months of the year after himself.'

'Turkmenistan. His name was Saparmurat Niyazov and he died in 2006.'

He wasn't showing off; he was just telling me a bit more about a place in which I'd shown interest. And I (a) couldn't remember any of the key facts in the radio item, not one, and (b) was seemingly no longer able to string two words together of any kind.

Evidently I have this flaw which provokes me to push myself away from people while wanting, at least consciously, to join in. You're probably thinking this is mad. Probably you find yourself seeing the point of view of most people you meet, or even vaguely agreeing with them, in the desire to be sociable, rather than to make life even more stressful for yourself, as I seem to do.

But assume just for a moment I'm not that weird. What if there's no such thing as the 'person you are' and we're all a collection of the various people we are in each relationship? You know the classic female dual-thingy, Madonna and whore. Well, I'm quite a few people, and several of them I definitely don't like. What's more, I know when my mother gets to this bit she'll be muttering, 'Nor do I, mate, nor do I.'

18 I Am Not Becoming Her 1: Let's Call the Whole Thing Off

Half-term. We're on holiday at the coast, where we have assembled at our usual café for elevenses. The children are slurping milkshakes. On the CD player, a classic track is playing by one of the great R&B groups of the 1970s, the Temptations, who combined socially conscious lyrics with killer rhythms. I go up to the counter to order more coffees. The man serving is young and good-looking. He starts making the coffees.

'Ah, "Cloud Nine"! You wouldn't remember this,' I say.

He smiles faintly.

'This record.'

The smile becomes ever so slightly fixed. Soon the coffees will be ready and I will go away and he can go back to serving normal people. People who don't use the word 'record'.

'It's about drugs, you know.'

The smile is set now. He watches the cups fill up.

'Two pounds eighty, please.'

I give him the money and retreat to our table.

'What were you on about over there?' says Peter.

'Nothing.'

He gives me one of his Looks, the one that means 'I hope you were only flirting and not complaining – about the speed of the service, or the size of the portions, or droning on in a manner likely to bring the marriage into disrepute.'

But of course I have been. And I have crossed a very major line. If only I hadn't done this. If I had at least stopped at the word 'record', or even stuck to my equally sad habit of saying 'the other day' when referring to something that happened in the 1980s, it would have been all right. I could have turned back. But pathetically trying to engage a handsome youth in a chat about the music of the 1970s – before he was even *born* – tells me that I have irrevocably crossed that line. I have begun turning into my mother.

In a fair world, that would mean I am becoming taller, better-looking and cleverer. But it doesn't.

I didn't think this would happen. Do I wear bright, home-made-looking clothes up to town?

Dance in front of my kids' friends? I don't *think* so. Besides, times have changed. Nowadays everyone is trendy. Children and adults listen to the same music, watch the same films, wear clothes from the same shops. The generation gap has narrowed and it's a tight squeeze. When I'm seventy and Lydia's thirty-five, we'll probably still be watching *Toy Story* together.

But there is Another Force at work that lurks in the space between me and my children. As I stand at the counter I realize I am, or soon will be, an Embarrassing Older Woman. My mother isn't, and wasn't, inherently embarrassing; she just became so by dint of (a) being a different generation and (b) being my mother. She also sang in the street.

I never sing. Peter sometimes does – only at home, but the children still stop him.

'Doe, a d—' is as far as he gets with their favourite song from *The Sound of Music* before one of them barks, 'Stop singing!'

And he has a really good voice. He sang the theme from *The Italian Job* to me once when I was on heavy-duty painkillers and ended up stuck on the loo for most of a weekend. There was nothing to choose between him and Matt Monro; in fact I prefer his version. I mean, surely the standard of the singing should count for something. Presumably Pavarotti's children didn't used to call out from the stalls, 'Stop, Daddy, you're so embarrassing!'

Or Darcey Bussell's children: 'Mu-um! It's like, in front of loads of *people*!'

So, singing or dancing in front of three people: embarrassing. In front of a thousand: fine.

My mother danced in front of my friends. Anything in front of your friends is potentially embarrassing, but she'd hear Stevie Wonder or David Bowie coming through the wall and would flock – she can single-handedly flock – through the door while waggling her head like the floor show in a cheap South African hotel. (I've never stayed in a cheap South African hotel; I just feel sure they have head waggling on the menu somewhere.) She was brought up in Scotland, where you could be sent to hell for swinging your hips on a Sunday, so God knows where she got it from. There was a Dutch Indonesian boyfriend just after the war whose sisters were apparently always lilting around the room in sarongs, so I guess we should blame them. Also, she has always set great store by being spontaneous, a free spirit swept up in the magic of the moment whom mere convention cannot tame. Hence the head waggling, which was enough to contend with, and this was before she discovered the joys of disco, when she began to combine languid arms with a kind of zigzagging, like Isadora Duncan dodging machine-gun fire.

So I know perfectly well the fate that, if I'm not very careful, awaits me. Yet some irresistible force compels me: my natural sense of rhythm. Or, as Lawrence puts it, my 'natural sense of being embarrassing'.

I have already been told off by Lydia for moving about to music in the car – i.e. swaying – and executing a few twirls to Earth, Wind & Fire, my favourite band from the 1970s, whose *Greatest Hits* I have recently rebonded with.

Then Peter's sister got remarried, and because thirty years ago she astutely made friends with the wife of a musician, there was a live band. It's not every day you get a six-piece jive ensemble in a south London dining room, and I felt compelled to make the most of it. Claire was there, with whom I enjoyed many girls' nights out in our remote youth. This, I realized, might be my last chance to dance in public, while the kids were still too young to protest. After all, the next time we hear music this old, we'll be in sheltered housing.

We glanced from side to side and, having established that Lawrence and Lydia were elsewhere, wiring into the canapés, fell into the routine from our 1970s disco days: think the Temptations but with floppier tummies. 'My Baby Just Cares For Me!' 'Choo-Choo Ch'Boogie'! 'Tequila'! We were in our element. We were in the wrong decade as well. But we didn't care – at least until I did a twist down to the floor and failed to twist up again.

Claire said, 'I can't do that. My knees won't stand it.'

'Er, nor will mine.'

She was caught last year dancing at a party – not by Leo, who at two hasn't yet learned the word 'embarrassing', but by her knee surgeon.

'What the hell was your knee surgeon doing at a *party*?'

'I dunno.'

'Is he following you?'

'It's the nearest I get these days to any interest from the opposite sex.'

Suddenly I felt a jab from an eight-year-old elbow.

'Mummy, stop doing that.'

'What, darling?'

'That stupid thing with your knees.'

'That's the Twist.'

'Well, it's embarrassing.'

Back in our kitchen: 'Mummy, do you *have* to do that?'

'Children, did you know I (*twirl*) once won a prize for my dancing?'

It was at the Rock Garden on a Monday night, but still.

'Yeah, you told us. Like, a million times.'

'You won a "record",' adds Lydia, to show she was paying attention and not, as I often contend, gazing into space.

Then Lawrence lifts his pen from his homework and says to Lydia, 'So who d'you think's the worse dancer, then? Mum or Dad?'

And Lydia answers, 'Dad, definitely.'

So that's all right.

Except it isn't, because we now have this thing with the words. It started a couple of years back, when Lawrence was eight. He had just got his first pair of roller blades – a pound in the school jumble sale, in case you think we're spoiling him – and I asked him if he wanted to skate to the park.

'*Blade*. It's *blading*, not "skating". Why can't you remember that?'

'Sorry! But really, it's the same thing, isn't it?'

One day, I get a chance to reverse the roles.

Lawrence turns ten, and we go on a tour of the car showrooms of Park Lane and Kensington, browsing among the Aston Martins and Ferraris, and in some cases even getting to sit in them. It's a perfect day out – free, and free from any kind of stress. We're just two pals together, mulling over the respective merits of the Maserati Quattroporte and the Lamborghini Gallardo.

As we stroll to the tube station, Lawrence says, 'Look, Mummy. Porsche Careera.'

And I say, 'It's *Carrera*.'

And he says, 'No, it *isn't*!'

'YES, IT IS!'

'No, it *ISN'T*!'

'YES, IT IS!!!!!'

Carrera *Caree-ra*, Caree-ra *Carrera*: let's call the whole thing off.

Then my friend Rebecca and I were in a clothes shop and I saw one of those little tiny evening jackets.

'Oh, look,' I said. 'A snug.'

As soon as I'd said it, I knew I meant *shrug*; a snug is a room in a pub. But it was too late. At least Rebecca just thought it was hysterical. But it was uncanny, as if my mother was speaking through me.

When I was fifteen, I bought 'Magic Mind', by

Earth, Wind & Fire, and she put her head round the door to listen.

'Is this Earth, Air, Fire & Water? They're very good, aren't they?'

'Mummy!'

'What? I like them!'

I mean, Earth, Air, Fire & Water? Come on! You might as well say *Love's Labour's Losing It*, or *Apocalypse Quite Soon*.

To be fair, mine was by no means the only offender. In 1983, the entire country spent what seemed an eternity under the spell of Frankie Goes to Hollywood and their hit single 'Relax'. At the height of it, my friend Joanna's mother, keen like mine to appreciate 'young taste', phoned her from the country.

'I do like that group, Freddie Goes to America.'

'Oh, *Mum* . . .'

'What?'

My friend Lucinda's mother was Oxford-educated and prided herself on her correct pronunciation. Lucinda would cringe as she saw certain words looming up in the conversation, such as 'pizza' and 'microwave', which her mother would insist on pronouncing with a short 'i'. Putting an LP on the 'steereo' also marked her out as one of the uncool generation, for whom these things were still exotic and new. It harked back to decimalization, when to be exposed as old and imminently obsolete, all you had to do was still be referring to 'new pence' five years after everyone else had stopped, or, going further back, 'electric light'. I imagine Tudor teenagers were similarly irritated by their parents asking for 'New World tubers' instead of potatoes, or maybe '*potahtoes*'. Come to think of it, the Gershwins' great work, which begins 'You say tomayto and I say tomahto', is surely just as brilliant an illustration of how the generations become alienated from each other as it is a love song.

And talking of songs, the latest craze among seven- to twelve-year-old girls, *High School Musical*, is currently sweeping the country in live, DVD and CD form. I mention this because I just met a man named Ed who described it as *High Street Musical*. It just doesn't have the same ring to it, does it? I didn't draw attention to it, though, apart from laughing and pointing in front of his friends.

And that brings us back to my tendency to say 'record'.

'Hey, you lot, we must get the new record by . . .'
'What's a *record*?'

Lawrence knows perfectly well what it is; this is his technique for training me out of saying it. With his current keenness on science, electric shock therapy can't be far off.

'Sorry, I mean CD. Download. Whatever.'

But perhaps I am getting off lightly. One day I fall into conversation with two women who work at the library, both of whom have teenage girls.

'I know when you get a coffee these days you're supposed to say "to go",' says the first one, 'but my father, their grandad, always says, "to take away, please" and this drives them wild!'

And her friend says, 'Oh yes! And my two won't let me say "latte".'

'Why? What should you say?'

'*Lah-tay*.'

'Don't be ridiculous,' I say. 'It's Italian, for God's sake!'

La-tte, *lah-tay*; lahtay, *la-tte* . . .

She says she then tries to prove her credentials by reminding them that she (a) actually speaks Italian and (b) even lived for a while in Italy. But her daughters don't care. They've stopped listening and, like, *whatever*.

I used to wonder why my friends weren't horrified by my mother's spontaneous leapings, then I realized it was because she wasn't *their* mother. It's hard-wired into the species. Darwin and Wallace clearly got this when they discovered the reason for apparently random mutations, namely that the off-spring are *embarrassed* to look like the parents. Hence the evolution of the frog, a creature that can breathe on land and in water, so wherever its mother is, it can be somewhere else.

Peter has another principle to impart, that the same is true in reverse.

'Other people's parents can be Cool.' he explains. 'One's own parents must never be Cool.'

When Lawrence and I were on the way to school recently and we bumped into a friend of his, the friend said hello in a funny voice and *I said hello in a funny voice back*. Lawrence was mortified. I decide not to tell Peter this.

'Of course,' he adds, 'far worse than being Uncool is trying to be Cool.'

'Of course, of course,' I say. 'Like, *der.*'

I remember the dad on Sports Day at the local nursery school who turned up clad from head to foot in yellow Lycra. Being a bit overweight, he looked like a pack of shrink-wrapped lemons. He then crouched right down for the start of the Fathers' Race – in itself a bit absurd with the spectators being mostly under five – sprang forward at the whistle and fell over.

But then Peter did pretty much the same thing as me. He addressed one of Lawrence's friends by the shortened version of his name, the one *Lawrence himself uses*. And Lawrence said he was being Really Embarrassing. I can't quote the boy's actual name, obviously; I don't want to make matters worse.

But then, matters already are worse, since I've begun picking up litter. Not *all* litter, just the bits that are distinctive enough and clean enough to touch. But it marks a definite degeneration down the Embarrassment Slope. Two years ago they didn't notice or care. Now we've all moved up a stage, them to the age of being embarrassed by my picking up litter, and me to the point of not caring what they think about my picking up litter.

When Peter was at school, parents had precious little opportunity to embarrass their offspring because it was boarding and visits were rare. However, because the school was a bit *progressive*, parents could be prone to unpredictable displays of individuality.

'There was a lord,' he recalls, 'who came to Open Day in a Land Rover . . .'

'What's wrong with *that*?'

'Different.'

'Er, OK . . .'

'And there was a boy who asked his father to park out of sight, because his car was so embarrassing.'

'What, really cheap and shabby?'

'A vintage Bugatti.'

Then there was Peter's friend James, whose parents decided to *cycle* to Open Day – which no one did in those days – arriving not only all red-faced and sweaty but in the equivalent for their generation of yellow Lycra: plus-fours.

My mother usually appeared at school dressed very well, but naturally the day that sticks in my mind is when she came to collect me in gold sandals and a floor-length kaftan.

'It was the 1970s' was her – not unreasonable – defence.

I foolishly mentioned this once to a girlfriend of my father's, who said, 'At least I've never gone to school in a *kaftan*.'

Coming from someone who used to wear a silver skirt and green tights, this was, I thought, a bit rich. As Jesus so very nearly said, 'Let she whose veil does not clash with her robe cast the first stone.'

And – except when it comes to yellow Lycra – I'm 100 per cent with him on that.

19 Stairway to Heaven

One weekend we go down to see her and discover fat white handrails on the staircase and a device like a stairlift in the bath: a present from social services.

Surely they've been put in the wrong house. It's an awful jolt, as if she's been recategorized by people who don't know her.

She hasn't said a word about these . . . architectural prosthetics, so I do my best not to react. She already has the weirdest bathroom in Britain – a long, thin room like a train corridor with bath, sink and lavatory all in a line; if two of you go in to brush your teeth you have to file out in reverse order. So a couple of handles and a chair that goes up and down in the water are hardly going to make it any worse. But this means there has been a major shift in status. Up until now we could pretend nothing had really changed; she's slower than me and I'm slower than Lydia and Lydia's slower than the boy in Year 6 who always wins everything. Everyone's slower than someone.

'They're just on loan,' she says.

'Oh, right.'

But we both know this is a technicality. She is never going to go up these stairs any faster than she does now.

This is independent, objective proof that she is old: my mother. Like a phone to which we've lost the charger, she is inexorably grinding to a halt. I don't know if she's ready for this, but I'm sure as hell not.

Given any warning I would never have accepted these 'aids', might even have let her fall rather than admit she needs them.

'They only come in white,' she adds. 'I asked.'

'No matt black, then?'

'Ha-ha, apparently not.'

She thinks I'll be bothered mainly by the aesthetics. And they are indisputably state rather than private accessories. But of course it's not that.

The handrails and the bath seat are now part of who she is. And what disconcerts me is that these people who I think don't know her actually know her better than we do.

By a spooky coincidence, I have recently slipped while getting into the shower and slammed my 'good' knee painfully against the edge of the bath. Is our troubled relationship expressing itself in some sort of weird, voodoo-ish way?

'Attention seeking,' says Peter, flicking the ibuprofen out of reach.

The next morning I have a bath in the weird long bathroom. And as I go to get out I reach for the handrail. The handrail! I recoil. I try to get up without it, but with my bad knees I daren't run the risk of slipping. The *handrail*. It echoes round my head like the infamous ejaculation by Lady Bracknell.

'A *HANDRAIL*?? To have one sore knee, Miss Calman, may be regarded as a misfortune. To acquire *two* looks like carelessness.'

I think of reproducing this for her when I get downstairs, but by the time I reach the kitchen, taking care not to touch the handrails, I have lost heart. She's getting old all right, and she's dragging me with her.

20 Trick or Treat

It's Halloween, which I've been dreading. It's hard up against Lydia's birthday and I already have enough to get stressed over without having to get sweets to hand out to scary youths demanding sugar with menaces, as happened last year, and the likelihood, if I don't answer, of egg on the door. The children are going out with Katarina, our former nanny and fifth family member, and I have to try quite hard not to let my humbuggishness spoil their fun. Also, it's six o'clock and they don't yet have anything to wear.

Of the many of my mother's characteristics I don't share, right at the top is the ability to whip up fairy wings, queen's crowns and witchs' hats in short order. It wasn't just that she could turn everyday household materials into gold; we always had the right stuff. I grew up knee-deep in huge paint tubes, coloured card and spray glue, since her whole bedroom-studio was an art room, where work and play fused together. Even the Rowntree's fruit gums in the kitchen cupboard weren't for eating, but to be scrambled at a moment's notice as jewels to stick on to crowns. There was nothing involving superior hand–eye coordination and a stapler that could faze her; whatever fate – or school – could throw at us, she was ready.

This was back when no one did trick-or-treating here, or even bothered with Halloween very much at all. But it was quite a big deal in Scotland, where she came from, so every year once we were old enough she invited our friends and any interested children who lived nearby to come up to the flat in their scariest disguises. Any who came unadorned – who lacked materials or whose parents didn't want mess in the house – she would sort out with green face paint or the spare witchs' hats she'd prepared with her trusty stapler and supply of black card. Then we'd all thunder down the stairs and troop through the streets to our friend Jane's place to squash into her tiny living room and listen to her mother tell ghost stories. The highlight was usually seeing the looks of incomprehension on the faces of the foreign students we encountered outside the university hall of residence on the way.

One year, as we were waiting for everyone to

arrive, Mum disappeared into the bathroom and came out a few minutes later, having painted an eye on her forehead.

'It's the Third Eye, which can see into the future,' she told us.

It was certainly convincing. The doorbell rang and she opened it to our first guest, a five-year-old boy who took one look at her, burst into tears and had to be taken home. My sister and I were impressed.

When we hit adolescence we naturally made sure not to mention the eye, since what had been awesome was now embarrassing, and we didn't want her to be reminded to do it again. The neighbourhood gatherings faded away, to be replaced, after Mum moved out, by one twenty-something party at which fake blood and wine got on to the furnishings and the sitting-room door was broken, inspiring us never to do it again. Anyhow, the thrill of whooping through the streets, baffling the students – i.e. the magic of being eight – could never be replaced.

Now I am living in the time of Trick or Treat, and am dressing up my own children. But my eyes are very much not lighting up at the thought of wrestling with black card; I will have to fake any confidence I appear to have when wielding the scissors and anyway I've left far too little time. The other big difference between me and my mother on these occasions is that I don't remember her barking at us to 'Stand *still*, for God's sake!' or saying, when they try to do any part of it themselves, 'Well, *that's* going to look crap.' She was an enabler, where I'm more of a – bossy old cow. Still, since the scariest part of their evening will almost certainly be my getting them ready, the trick-or-treating can only be a success.

I have suggested to Lydia that in the interests of speed she revive last year's black-cat outfit: black mask, black tights with length of black fluffy stuff sewn on the back, and what Peter calls my single person's black polo neck that I used to wear before I met him – and eyeliner whiskers. But she doesn't want to, precisely because black cat is so last year. Then her friend Daphne turns up as 'Draculina' in black velvet gown, sexy make-up and little drawn-on pointy teeth – a vampire with the emphasis on the vamp – and so Lydia wants to be that. She gets on the black tights and as I'm painting on her red lipstick and teeth I have a sense of something very like déjà vu.

Lawrence is meant to be going as Death, though we can't find his scythe. I've been tripping over it all year of course, among the coats and bags and cricket bats, then on the one day we *need* a six-foot pole with a huge blade on top, it's not there. Somehow we find another broom handle – quite an achievement in a house where no one does any sweeping – and by some piece of luck there's a tiny bit of silver spray left in the can. Then, just after we've spent forty minutes getting the silver cardboard blade to stay on the pole, he says he doesn't want to be Death any more, he wants to be a zombie, and can I paint his face with red and black scars.

The déjà vu feeling gets stronger. Then I remember the year my mother painted the eye on her forehead. And I feel a strange force compelling me to do the same.

This is a surprise, as when someone who's never been to Germany goes under hypnosis and starts suddenly speaking German. Very appropriately for Halloween, I am feeling ever so slightly possessed.

I go to the mirror and start painting the eye, the brush moving automatically in deft strokes. The children stop fighting over the black face paint and stare at me, transfixed. As I finish it off with a nice bright green iris, the phone goes – Lawrence's mate Tristan, asking if they can meet up en route. Lawrence answers it and tells him, for once abandoning his 'casual' voice and letting enthusiasm creep in; 'Hey, guess what? My mum's painted this really cool eye on her forehead!'

He doesn't often describe anything I've done as cool. Actually he doesn't ever. This is *amazing*. Suddenly I realize that Halloween is really quite fun after all, and instead of hiding upstairs in the bedroom with the small telly on, I pour myself a drink, fill a bowl with sweets, wave off Katarina and the children and prepare to open the door to all comers.

I give out sweets and party poppers to small children and groups of teenage girls in minimal costumes, who thank me politely before scampering away. It's too dark for the littler ones to see the eye immediately, so I bend down and intone, 'Look into my magic eye . . . It can see all your bad deeds, so you'd better be good . . .'

This blend of wicked witch and Father Christmas works almost too well on the younger ones, so, remembering my mother's effect on that five-year-old all those years ago, I make sure to smile broadly at the same time. Then I realize I am actually enjoying myself. The only fly in the wine, as it were, is that she isn't here with me.

Over the next few days I keep thinking about Lawrence's comment to his friend, and how happy I

would be if there was something of my own invention, as opposed to my mother's, that he thought was
cool. Then it's Lydia's birthday and, as if guided
once more by an invisible hand, I find myself making
crêpe-paper flowers.

My mother taught me how to do these so long
ago I can't even remember the first time. The last
time I know *she* did them was for my father's sixtieth
birthday. He had a marquee, and she just offered,
quite casually, to make some to twine round the
supports.

'What, your mother made them for your father's
birthday!' says Peter, who has never quite got to
grips with families like mine, which extend, rather
than shrink, after divorce.

But they often did things like this for each other,
or even together. When I had to dress up as a
European currency for a day at school celebrating
our entry into the Common Market, the two of them
got together to draw one side each of a pound note
that they attached to two of those horizontal poster
hangers for me to wear, like a sandwich board. They
spent hours on it, just as if it was a real design job,
enjoying a bit of light-hearted competition over
whose side was the more realistic. She teased him
over his inferior drawing skill, and he acknowledged

her superior ability while laughingly defending some cartoonish graphic he had done that didn't really work at all, such as his attempt at a likeness of the Queen.

Now it is Lydia's ninth, and Peter and I are just snapping at each other about the amount of work we've given ourselves – ridiculous, when you consider it's six girls and a face painter – when Lawrence, who's been allowed a mate of his own to stay, breezes in.

'Hey, Tom. Look at these really cool flowers my mum's made.'

And Tom, who isn't *that* impressed, as he is after all a ten-year-old boy as opposed to a middle-aged woman, mutters something vaguely positive and in a moment they are up in his room, making the ceiling shake by leaping on and off the old sofa. But I remain in the moment. That's the second time Lawrence has praised something I've done as Cool, and both times it's been something I've copied from her!

Considering I can't remember what I had for breakfast this morning, I have no idea how on earth I still know how to make those flowers. It's like one of those old routes you have in your head that you don't think about consciously, but that when you get

to a certain point you just follow. Without any conscious thought involved, I cut the petals out of
magenta crêpe paper, stretching them to get the
right tension so they curve outwards from the middle, and holding them just right so they overlap like
rose petals for an authentic effect. (Keeping them
bound together in the middle is the hardest bit.)

There is no having to concentrate on the next bit
of the recipe, as with say baking a cake; the process
just seems to be stored in my hands. I remember my
mother once telling me of a great doctor she read
about who, while doing his training in a psychiatric
hospital, came across a former shoemaker. He would
walk the corridors making these odd, repetitive hand
movements, and everyone thought it was evidence
of his madness. Then one day this doctor copied the
movement, nodding as if to say, 'Yes, that makes
sense.' And the man then explained that he was
demonstrating part of the process of how to make
shoes. It was the only way he had left to show them
who he was.

I carry on lingering in the hall, nipping back and
forth to the kitchen to top up my red wine. The
doorbell rings again and there are two small children, a ghost and a devil, looking sweetly up at me.

'*Blood*, anyone?' I hear myself saying. The children look back at their father, uncertain. But it is what she would say, if she were here, and so it feels right.

21 I Am Not Becoming Her 2: Caramba! The Girl Has Hidden the Knob!

In our old house, Peter and I did a little thing as a security measure when we went out. We left the radio on. The house was in a street which generally suffered no more crime than the occasional broken car window, but it made us feel more relaxed. Also, you entered it through a tiny courtyard garden with its own door, so even if anyone suspected the place was empty, it was impossible to tell. There was a minor drawback, which was that I occasionally forgot I'd put the radio on, and I once came through the garden to hear what sounded like a woman being beaten up. I cowered outside the back door for a full five minutes before realizing it was Radio 4, and the domestic violence story that was then running on *The Archers*.

My mother has her own security measures. She

doesn't leave the radio on; rather, the opposite. She's inherited her own mother's fear of rogue electrical fires, so switches everything off when she goes out, and lately not just then but while people are still there. A room only has to be empty for about thirty seconds before it is plunged into darkness. If you're in the kitchen and nip out to get something from the car, or even the hall, she immediately comes in behind you and turns off the lights. And having read somewhere that 0.001 per cent of domestic fires are caused by spontaneously combusting television sets, she not only turns it off but unplugs it as well. This wouldn't be such a nuisance were it not for her other habit of constantly putting things in front of things, so to reactivate the telly after a night of dormancy means having to climb over the sofa and move two wobbling, shadeless lamps so you can get to the socket.

Years ago, when she moved out and my sister and I were left to share the flat, we thought it would be sensible to prepare a code word in case one of us was captured by baddies. Our father's income was far from being in the ransom category, but years of reading *Bunty* had convinced us we needed a strategy in case Colombian bandits broke into our second-floor flat and got one of us in a death grip while the other was out.

'If one of us rings up and the other is in danger,' we decided, 'the baddies will tell the one they've got to say everything's OK.'

'So we need a word that means "Help, I'm being held hostage!" but only to us.'

So we decided to copy our hero Captain Kirk and borrow the term he used whenever he'd beamed down to a planet and got into a bit of bother and wanted to covertly tell the crew on the *Enterprise* to come and get him.

'Condition green: all's well,' we'd say, because two sisters in 1980s Bloomsbury would say that. And the bandits would never notice and shout, 'Caramba! The girl is trying to send a secret signal!' and then strangle us.

My mother, meanwhile, having moved out to the country, was anxious not to tip off potential burglars to the fact that she lived alone. The police tell us that housebreakers target properties with easy access or windows accidentally left open, but not according to her. My mother is convinced that they choose their marks by randomly going through the phone book and ringing people in the hope of hearing an answerphone message with an 'I' on it instead of 'We'. But just changing the 'I' to 'We' was too straightforward. So she invented a fictitious boyfriend whose name she added to her own. She named him 'Ian Calder', which for a Freudian like her surely had Oedipal overtones as they were her father's first two names. If her friends thought she'd secretly taken up with a man from her home country, possibly even from her old life before my dad, they were too polite to say. And because her adherence to correct syntax made it imperative that she word the outgoing message correctly, it came out as: *'Neither Pat McNeill nor Ian Calder can come to the phone right now. So please . . .'* and so on.

I hoped that potential burglars would draw the conclusion that anyone obsessional enough to start a sentence like that would be bound to have a lot of locks.

Eventually the phantom partner was retired and the message changed to: *'We can't take your call at the moment, so if you'd like to, um, leave a message, we'll phone you back.'* The *um* drives me mad. It's as though she can't remember what she's doing or is being held hostage by bandits from *Bunty* comic and the *um* – from someone so supremely articulate – is her only way of alerting the police.

Meanwhile, back in London, my sister moved out to live with her boyfriend and I was left alone. Security was not an issue. The flat was not only on the second floor but had a two-inch-thick front door and was pretty much impregnable. However, I had written a book about life as a single female and one evening had a call from a man who asked me out. He said he was a solicitor, which if he wasn't lying made him far more respectable than the men I actually was dating at the time, but I figured that it was as well if complete strangers who'd just been reading about my preferences in foreplay didn't have my home address. So I took myself out of the telephone directory and off the public extract of the electoral roll.

That was the sensible course to take, and nothing like the weird rigmaroles practised by my mother.

Then, about two years before Peter and I moved into our present house, we were burgled. They got, among other things, my computer, and while I did have a back-up disk, I didn't like the feeling of vulnerability it left. We got an alarm and upgraded a couple of locks. But I also invented a little extra measure which I've carried on where we are now. Peter thinks it's just like something my mother would do. I'm going to tell you what it is, so you can see that I'm not like her at all.

The handle of my study door happens to be quite loose. In fact, it's completely loose. I got shut in once when it fell off and I had to open the door with pliers. It gave me an idea. The door has a lock but no key, but I've got something better than that. Now, whenever I go out, I remove the handle from the outside and hide it.

Genius, eh? It has the added benefit of keeping out children and only causes a problem when Sophie, my long-suffering PA, comes round to find I've put it in a different place. I used to put it in the little cupboard in the upstairs bathroom, but the cupboard is underneath the sink rather than on the wall, and when my knee started to get worse I didn't like the bending. So I started hiding it among the towels. I'm only telling you this so you know why I moved it. It's not as though I imagine that someone might be magically watching me up there in a windowless second-floor room and seeing where I put it. I'm not *that* strange. Anyway, if you're reading this as a potential burglar, obviously I have moved it again since then. So don't think you can get my stuff.

The point about security measures is that even the faintly odd ones do have a purpose. My mother's need to turn all her bathroom products round so that you can't read the labels is just pointless and weird. They don't even look nice, because instead of seeing a perfectly acceptable word like 'lotion' or 'cleaner', you get a row of panels of small print – the bits that say 'not to be drunk by unsupervised children' – and EU-approved hazardous-liquids warning symbols. In the past I used to turn them all round again while I was waiting for the bath to fill, but now I'm cured of that and confine myself to rehanging the lopsided dressing gowns instead. She has about eight, all hung by one shoulder rather than their collars, so that they look like a small crowd of people who've all pulled one shoulder, waiting for the osteopath. As for becoming like her, I don't do anything weird with my bathroom products or my dressing gowns, of which I have a perfectly normal two. Sometimes when I'm by the cooker I line up the lids and bodies of all my glass storage jars, so that the seams in the glass go the same way. Then I turn them slightly so that the seams aren't visible from where I stand. But that's not weird; that's just being neat.

22 I Am Not Becoming Her 3: Mission to Explain

One of my mother's quirks is her way of introducing people. Most of us will add some detail or other about someone to give the other person a kind of foothold with which to begin their conversation. At a wedding, for example, one might say, 'This is Tim, the one she chucked before you.'

Or at a funeral: 'This is Jerry. The old bastard owed money to him too,' thus giving the introducees a firm footing on which to base an acquaintance.

My mother goes one further, or rather two or three further. She delivers a detailed biography of each person, covering the main points of their marriages and career to date, in a well-shaped speech worthy of inclusion in any professional handbook, which leaves the subjects nothing to say except, 'Yup, that pretty much covers it,' before moving on to someone else.

It's all part of her mission to explain.

Years and years ago, when the local garage charged her lots of money for pretending to repair her Mini, she told them she was going to have it inspected by the AA. This was explaining her position, so as to be fair. By an amazing coincidence the car was stolen the very next day.

She is afraid that people cannot always manage with the paltry information provided for them by the universe and their own senses, and believes that her role, therefore, is to step in and fill the breach. If she does not, they may misunderstand something, or make a mistake, or come to some other harm. This is why she had to tell me I mustn't sit under the bump in the kitchen ceiling – and indeed I don't sit there any more, though not for the reason she thinks – and why she has to stand behind Peter and describe the various disorders to which the blinds/locks/curtain rails have succumbed over the years, while he is actually fixing them.

Needless to say, I am nothing like this. I introduce people with the barest wisp of information, just enough to whet the curiosity, and I never stand behind someone telling them how to perform a simple task.

There is only a teensy weensy explaining thing I

do when someone invites us for dinner or whatever and we can't make it, but all women do that. As my friend Emmie used to put it, 'I'm not free tomorrow and I'll tell you why,' before launching into a detailed list of her commitments for the next several days. Actually I have a male friend who does it as well, in that 'I'm so busy and stressed' way that makes me want to slap him across the head. I don't do that of course, I just give the person a little bit of background by way of explaining why we're not free, along the lines of: 'I'm really sorry, but we're already going out to this thing, with these people who – well, you remember that nursery that Lawrence *didn't* go to? The one near the library. Well, the woman I met at the interview . . .'

While Peter stands behind me, hissing, 'You – don't – have – to – *ex – plain*!'

When I was in my twenties I went to live with a boyfriend for a while in Dubai, which then was just as it is now, only with fewer shopping malls and more sand. While most of my friends were shocked that I would even contemplate setting foot in an Islamic sheikhocracy and would almost certainly be jailed for having my skirt the wrong length, my mother was worried about how I would learn to drive on the right-hand side of the road.

'What kind of car does he have?' she said. 'Because you're going to need to read the manual.'

Driving is one of those processes which definitely does not improve with the addition of more information. But she's compelled to provide these signposts, instructions and footnotes to remind us of how much more complicated the world is than we realize. One night she rang me and I said I was going to a neighbour's birthday party.

'I hope you're not going to drink and drive,' she said. Oddly enough I wasn't, not least because the house was only ten doors up. This is even weirder when you think that, twenty years ago, she used to let me smoke.

'How do you think I cope the rest of the time?' I said.

For several decades now I've been able to drive, change plugs and even get my finger in my nostril without looking. Are there Child Years, d'you think, like Cat Years? She counts one for every seven I've actually lived.

As for telling people how to perform simple tasks, as I say, I don't do that either. Peter *says* I do. He makes breakfast most mornings and if I so much as *look* at the frying pan he thinks I'm telling him what to do. Obviously now and then I have to just interject a wincy little observation, like, 'If you put the bacon and eggs into the large pan instead of two small ones, we'd only have to wash the one.'

And when he makes soup he sautés the vegetables in the frying pan, *then* transfers them into the saucepan to add the stock, which, as I sometimes do have to point out, is just ridiculous. I tell him, 'Why don't you just do the whole thing in one pan?'

And he gets really annoyed. But that doesn't count. And besides, the so-called micro-management that he finds so exasperating when I do it is miraculously transformed into an endearing little foible when it comes from her. I shouldn't complain. Let's do as he says and look on the bright side. He is after all the only man on the planet who wants his wife to be more like her mother.

23 Dear Mrs Bumtrinket

When Lydia was six, she made a tiara for her Barbie doll out of paper in the shape of a swan. It had a tiny swan's head at the front which snaked up on its thin neck between two tiny wings, creating a classic triangular, tiara shape.

I mention this not because I'm a proud mother – which of course I am – but because it is a very particular talent of Lydia's granny. I have a limited amount of ability in that area – I can do a passable cardboard crown or crêpe-paper flower, and Lawrence is no slouch with a pencil, but Lydia has the hand–eye gene. My mother adored her doll's house so much as a child that she carried on redesigning the rooms and making things for them right into her teens. And when I watch Lydia knitting little scarves for her teddies – with no input at all from me – I can see the DNA at work. She has also inherited my mother's dreaminess. When I'm saying, 'Lydia! Did you hear me?' for the fifth time, I am uncomfortably aware that I sound like my grandmother, who, according to my mother, nagged her constantly. I can plead one mitigating factor: at least in this family showing artistic tendencies is not regarded as pathological.

I grew up, as you do, thinking my parents were pretty typical. Didn't all children get home-made birthday cards and painting sessions on the floor with giant bottles of paint and a choice of five sizes of brush? Wasn't it quite normal to have entire cupboards full of tinsel, glitter, coloured acetate, A3 card, spray-on glue and felt squares in thirty different colours? Didn't everyone's mum come home with carrier bags full of cloth scraps collected from the doorways of fashion wholesalers, for making doll's house doll's clothes? Didn't they all get a mad light in their eyes when they thought they'd found the ideal thickness of leatherette for the shoes? And when other girls became obsessed with Elizabeth I after Glenda Jackson played her on TV, didn't their mothers make them a collage picture of her, complete with starched ruff, pearls in the classic Tudor arrangement and heavily jewelled gown?

Apparently not.

The art materials were used by both my parents for their work, but there wasn't much of a line between that and everything else. We were even allowed to draw next to them while they worked.

Peter thinks I don't appreciate this, but he's wrong. There's a limit to how often you can say, 'Ooh! What an amazing early life I had.'

But that doesn't mean I don't get it.

On a shelf in my study are three tiny letter boxes made out of old Sainsbury's spice pots, the twist-off lids painted black, the body of the pot red. They are decorated with 'ER', just like the real ones, and have tiny 'Collection Times' written on little panels. Each also has a rectangular slot, about one centimetre by three millimetres, for posting. And inside each box are several handwritten letters, on paper about two to three centimetres long.

My favourite of these is headed 'Narkover School, Hants'. It says:

Dear Mrs Bumtrinket,*

I very much regret to inform you that your son
Claude has not shown the improvement in his conduct,
nor his work, that we had hoped for, and
notwithstanding your magnificent gift of six onyx bidets

* The name of Gerald Durrell's boat in *My Family and Other Animals*.

for the use of the Governors, I have no alternative but to ask you to remove him from the school. I enclose, with regret, the bill for extras incurred last term.

   Yours faithfully
   PR Foulenough (Capt. Ret'd)

You then unfold the tiny bill:

Membership fees of newly revived Hellfire Club . . . £80
Gambling debts . . . £3,428
Fines levied on school after discovery of hemp
   plantation in school greenhouse . . . £200
Matron's abortion . . . £150

In another minuscule envelope is a voucher for '£5 off your next diamond tiara' courtesy of 'Splosh' washing powder.

I was in my early teens when she did these: old enough to know what an abortion was, but young enough to get a thrill from opening the tiny mail. Actually, the thrill has never gone.

We got the tiny postboxes in our stockings. Christmas was when my mother's imagination really got to flex its muscles. The year after the postboxes, she made little suitcases from matchboxes, painted black and brown to look like those old-fashioned leather ones with reinforced corners. They were dotted with tiny labels naming the places – Paris, Skye, Alderney – we'd been, and had tiny wire carrying handles. She cut the matchboxes open laterally, the way you slice a bun, and did something clever with the edges so that they could open and close. I have preserved the little postboxes for over thirty years, but the matchbox suitcases are gone, departed on unknown journeys of their own. I do, though, still have one of many matchbox chests of drawers she made, from six glued together in a double stack of three, with each drawer front painted a different colour and tiny brass fasteners for handles.

I've never made mini-postboxes. The most I've managed is a small letter from the Chief Tooth Fairy apologizing for staffing problems, i.e. Peter going to bed one time and forgetting to give Lawrence his pound. But the style of her present-giving, and the adherence to fairness, I have carried on without even thinking about it. The tradition of unbirthday presents, for example, was introduced to pre-empt tears when we were too young to cope with having nothing to open while the birthday sister had loads. The very first one, you could say, was the home-made wedding outfit I got when Claire was born. After that, the rule was that the non-celebrant received two or three unbirthday presents of demonstrably lower value than their sister's. This worked every year except for Claire's seventh, when Mum gave us both watches, leading to furious complaints. Remembering this, I try to make sure never to aggrieve one child by being over-generous to the other, appreciating, as I go about it, what a narrow line she had to tread.

The other practice I have upheld is cutting out a large 8 or 9, or whichever number it is, the night before their birthdays and taping it to the kitchen wall. This is a slightly more mundane version of her ritual: she always cut our numbers out of coloured tissue paper and stuck them on the bedroom window so that when we woke up and drew the curtains the light would shine through. Claire and I were so enamoured of this moment, when the curtains were opened and the new age revealed, that one year, with much whispering and hissed exhortations not to tear the tissue, we returned the favour.

'Mummy! Draw the blinds! Draw the blinds!' we squealed until, still groggy with sleep, for it was probably about six a.m., she pulled the cord to be confronted by a huge, bright red forty-four. She laughed; it would never have occurred to us that she could react otherwise.

After my father died in 1994, there was a series of sinking moments, like going down too quickly in a lift. One of the worst was when I noticed the shoebox I kept his letters in was full and carefully labelled a new one, before realizing it would never be filled. I'm not sure I won't do the same thing with my mother, except that this time I am better prepared. Having some distance between us has, I think, enabled me to appreciate the letters, pictures and cards on their own terms. When my father was alive, I expended a lot of energy trying to limit his influence on me, to resist the overwhelming tide of his love. It was almost only when his physical presence was gone that I was able finally to love him freely, without fear of being consumed. With her I have space to breathe, and in that space I can admire her talent with something approaching clarity. And I know exactly what I am going to miss.

I will miss not just her letters but the envelopes, with their distinctively illuminated '1st' in the top left-hand corner – snow lying on it in winter, or an umbrella over it to keep off spring showers. Often there is also a seasonal bird, with rainhat, wellies or sunglasses depending on the weather at the time of posting.

I keep them all in their shoeboxes in the storage chest she painted for me which has pride of place in my study. The lid is adorned with trompe-l'oeil objects painted to look as they would if scattered over the top of my desk: pens, an ashtray full of paperclips, a pencil from my favourite Glasgow hotel, a half-eaten bar of Cadbury's Dairy Milk, the end of a sandwich on a napkin with the logo of my favourite sandwich bar, my first two books, a bowl of tortelloni, some 'scribbles' by the children when they were small and, peeping out from under all those, the top of the letter I got from Channel 4 in 1992 commissioning my sitcom. My only regret is that, in my study, it does not get as wide an audience as it deserves.

And I am preparing a place on the main bookshelf in the sitting room, for the book she wrote and painted for me when I was five. *The Girl Who Had Stripes* is a full-size, full-colour story about a girl called Susie who wakes up one morning not with spots or blotches but stripes. Her parents take her to every kind of specialist, try every medicine, to no avail. Eventually they go on holiday to Scotland, where Susie sets off exploring one day and meets a caterpillar who takes her to the cottage of an old woman called Granny Mutchie. Granny Mutchie is not fazed by stripes. She has cured all sorts of skin complaints in her time including tartan. She mixes up a strange potion in her cauldron, throwing in, among other things, robin's breast feathers and violets and puts it into a giant bottle. Susie climbs into it and all the colours of the stripes disappear from her skin and get absorbed into the liquid. Then Granny Mutchie pours it away and the stripes swirl down the street, eventually forming those rainbow puddles you think are made from petrol. I had the book once, but it found its way back to her place. When I find it this time, though, I'm hanging on to it. It's an absolutely wonderful piece of work and I miss the happy ending.

24 You Don't Know How Lucky You Are 2: The Baum Identity

One weekend we're at her place. The children are outside playing and Peter is checking the oil in her car and being Marvellous, so it's just her and me in the house. We're drinking coffee and talking about something quite mundane, like how quickly the London squirrels demolished the bowl of spring bulbs she gave me for my birthday. She offers to get me some more and suggests this time I cover them in netting. I like talking about the minutiae of gardening. The details are like little footholds that help to keep us on course and away from any steep drops. I relax. But then there's a small shift in territory; somehow we veer off our theme and the subject of my father comes up. And suddenly she announces, 'Julianne said he was very disappointing in bed, you know.'

Aargh! As it is a complete change of subect she

has had to swerve the conversation round a huge great corner to get it in, like someone manoeuvring a grand piano into a very small flat. And I'm now stuck with it forever. I'm constantly forgetting things, from interest rates to the baby-sitters' holiday dates, but hey, you can bet I'll remember this.

It's not as though it's just happened either; my father's old girlfriends don't make a habit of unexpectedly popping up out of the undergrowth to rake over my father's sexual history, and certainly not anywhere near my mother. This was over twenty-five years ago back in London; a girl called Julianne rented a room in the house opposite. It was long after they were divorced and I remember almost nothing about her, except that she was a vegan with gappy teeth. I certainly didn't know they'd had a fling. And I feel that, on a need-to-know basis, I really, really don't need to know.

'She came round for coffee one day,' says my mother. 'And said he wasn't up to much "in that department", you know.'

What were they doing having coffee anyway? It reminds me of when I was on holiday in Greece just before I met Peter. I went for a walk with a perfectly nice-seeming man who suddenly put his willy in my hand. (I gave it back.)

'Why are you telling me this?' I say. 'Jesus!'

She shrugs, as if to say, 'What can you do?' and I leave the room with that awful Snakes and Ladders feeling coursing round my system, made all the more unnerving because the game is unequal; only she has sight of the board.

And, of course, Peter has missed the moment yet again.

On the drive back I say, 'Just listen to this,' and I tell him.

'Oh my God!' he says.

'It's like those extra loud traffic reports that suddenly burst into the middle of programmes on the car radio. I never know when it's going to happen.'

'Well, just tune out then.'

'She knows perfectly well what she's saying. She just wants to make me squirm. I can't stand it!'

He's not shocked, he's amused. He relishes these unscheduled revelations. He thinks his Mission on Earth is to get me to appreciate how wonderful she is.

On the basis of their shared belief, namely that a person can say whatever they like as long as it's not boring, they have formed a mutual admiration society. Also, Peter lost his own mother in childhood, and my mother loves surrogates. It irks her some-

what that, despite this early tragedy, he is emotionally quite stable with no need of fixing, but she's
prepared to overlook that. Other people's children
see only the good in you, with none of that annoying
blame and anger to get in the way. So with this, and
his DIY *and* conversation skills, he is literally the
ideal male. He has one fault – he's married to me.
But then nobody's perfect.

'A mother who's never boring! You don't know
how lucky you are.'

I know. Other people's mothers who live in the
country talk about the neighbour's dog getting in
again and trampling the roses, or the awful woman
who's taken over the village fête committee, how
rude everybody is these days, and how much they
miss Mrs Thatcher. They switch on the TV and
complain about the presenters' clothes, or hair, and
how all these new programmes are so violent; why
can't they bring back *Inspector Morse*? Whereas she
said when he rang her one evening, 'Lovely to hear
from you, but I'll have to be quick. I'm just watching
Bladerunner: The Director's Cut.'

On one of Peter's first visits there with me, the
three of us watched *Mad Max* together and smoked
a joint. Well, she didn't have any, but she told us to
go ahead. He'd never been out with anyone before

whose mother allowed them to smoke dope yet wasn't an ageing hippy.

'I think I might like it,' she said. 'But I don't really want to take up smoking.'

That statement is characteristic; she has no problem with the idea of cannabis in principle, but doesn't want to muck up her lungs. She's no Groovy Mum, still living the 1960s dream with an Isle of Wight Festival poster in the lavatory and a rusting Dormobile in the garden overrun by mice. Nor is she an Eccentric Artist Mum in paint-spattered overalls and big earrings, who drank with John Osborne and sat for Lucian Freud. She is eccentric, and she is, though she never uses the word, an artist. But she isn't an Eccentric Artist. To be that would be predictable, would mean she could be categorized. And if there's one thing you can say for sure about her, it's that she doesn't conform to any of the rules of nonconformity. And that's all fine; I just can't cope with this level of – unpredictability.

He brakes and, as we're at a red light, looks at me.

'But at least she's *interesting*,' he says, in the tone adults employ when saying, 'Sprouts are full of vitamins.'

'Oh, and interesting beats everything, does it?'

'You know what I mean. She's never dull.'

'So what? I would love, just once, to turn up and have a normal conversation, without having some horrendous bloody – revelation – shoved down my throat. I mean, come on! How would you like it if it was your mother?'

I never met his mother but I'm pretty sure she wasn't given to peppering the conversation with remarks about his father's sexual technique.

'I grew up in a pebble-dash semi . . .'

'Oh, here we go.'

'And – like many people, may I say – I wouldn't have minded parents as unusual as yours.'

'You don't know what other people want. You had lovely parents.'

'Yes, but all that creativity you had, all that dressing up and leaping around to music and going to Ronnie Scott's for your eleventh birthday . . .'

This is true. My dad met Ronnie and asked if he could bring me, and Ronnie said he didn't care what age I was, so long as I didn't get drunk and interrupt the performance.

'You always take the piss out of me for that.'

'Yes, but you know I don't mean it.'

It's not just my father's image that gets a tarnishing. She takes others' apart too. Sometimes she identifies them while claiming not to, which at least provides some light relief.

'The wife of an estate agent in the village, whom you don't know . . .'

And my sister, if she's there, will say, 'Jane.'

And my mother will look at her, staggered by her incredible powers of deduction.

'Well, there is only one estate agent in the village, so . . .'

Then, when she's trying to be discreet about someone she knows quite well, it's even funnier.

'A retired church organist, whom you don't know . . .'

And my sister will say, 'Er, Michael. Obviously.'

Actually, even the ultra-sharp Claire did once get caught out when it transpired that this small community was in fact harbouring *two* retired organists, one of whom she had indeed not met. The irony is that when Mum thinks she's disguising their identities, the so-called secrets are usually incredibly trivial, but when she makes no attempt at all the revelations can be really quite major.

In a different village, which you don't know . . . we used to spend weekends and holidays. My sister was still very small and I often used to play with

Rebecca,* the vicar's daughter. The vicarage was at the top of our lane and had a weeping willow on the lawn low enough to climb and where, taking it in turns to be pilot and co-pilot, Rebecca and I played 'jets'. When we burst, hot and panting, through the back door into the cool kitchen, her mother would give us lemonade in glasses decorated with red squiggles, or ice lollies, which I wasn't allowed at home. She wore patterned, full-skirted dresses and an apron, and if we complained that we were bored would say, 'Then let's put on our thinking caps!'

She really was that wholesome. Or so I thought.

'I used to love playing there,' I said to my mother one evening about two decades later. 'Is the weeping willow still there?'

She thought for a moment.

'Of course you know Barbara was an alcoholic.'

'What? No! Really?'

I'd only asked about the tree.

'Of course! It was well known.'

Being preoccupied with lemonade and ice lollies at the time, I had smelled nothing more illicit in their larder than cake.

---

* Not her real name, obviously.

'And he was Jewish.'

'*Jewish?*'

'Of course! With a name like Baum,* what did you think?'

'I didn't think anything; I was eight.'

She looked at me as if at thirty I had just heard there was no Father Christmas.

'He converted to Christianity.'

I felt suddenly protective of the poor Baums, their identity abruptly demolished in this casual way.

'And John and Rebecca were adopted.'

Their cover blown, she sat back expectantly. I immediately wished I could restore them to their previous status as a proper vicar's family.

'Wow,' I said. 'I never imagined.'

'Well, you must have noticed they didn't look like him.'

Since they were sandy-haired and freckled and he was bald, I hadn't expected them to. I felt obliged to ask something, to show an interest.

'How did you know? About the drinking.'

'Oh, it was all round the village. But the adoption she told me about in private.'

---

* Not their real surname either. I mention this because Peter thought I might not change it.

'Wow,' says Peter, when I am finished. But he is not unsettled at all, whereas I continue thinking about the Baums, haunted by their freckled faces, the mother's cheery voice that apparently wasn't, and the father's unreadable eyes behind his pebble glasses.

'But you know, every community has its secrets,' he points out. 'When I was growing up in Sheffield there was a grown-up brother and sister who lived in our road. Together.'

'And?'

'We always knew there was something odd about them.'

'Oh, for God's sake. Anyway, you said *secrets*. That's just my point.'

At around the same time as I knew Rebecca Baum, I had a friend at school called Phoebe.* Her mother, Muriel,† had a sculpture studio and often invited me round to play with the leftover bits of clay. A few years back, in adulthood, I was recalling these idyllic play sessions in their big house near Hampstead Heath.

'Muriel told me she had never had an orgasm, you know,' my mother announced.

---

* Whose name I have obviously also changed.
† Ditto.

'God! Do you have to? I mean, is it *really*—'

'Completely frigid! Can you imagine that?'

Well, yes I can. It's not entirely unheard of. Outing Muriel, a rich hippy in tie-dyed T-shirts, served no purpose. Was she jealous of my pottery lessons with her, or was it the big house and state-of-the-art studio? Thank God Phoebe and I lost touch decades ago when we went to different schools, so I didn't have to face her with the burden of my secret knowledge. Even thinking about Muriel now, while telling Peter, provokes a stab of reflected guilt, as if I were the mother of a criminal passing the scene of his crime.

'It's awful the way you can't keep secrets,' I told her prissily.

'I can't edit what I say!'

'You can,' I shot back, 'and you should!'

'Oh, there are lots of things you don't know,' she said.

'Well, good.'

There was a pause, unfortunately not long enough for me to get out of the room.

'I've never told you, for instance, about the time two women you knew rang me to say they were extremely concerned about the number of boyfriends you had.'

Peter is quiet, as we drive along. Then he says, 'Ah.'

'Never mind the irony,' I say. 'Sometimes, if I had to choose between the interesting, creative childhood I had and a dull one just with unconditional approval . . .'

'You wouldn't.'

'I might. Give it all up, just to be straightforwardly loved.'

'What you've had is very special. Trust me.'

'You don't know.'

'Well, even so. Your mother is an amazing woman and I won't hear a word against her.'

He's doing his winsome smile; he's decided now is just about all right for him to try and tease me out of this.

'Then this relationship is over. Leave the car now.'

'It's my car.'

'Then – you can stay.'

He may adore my mother, but as I say, nobody's perfect.

25 I Am Not Becoming Her 4: STs in Space

Lawrence is off school with a sore throat and temperature so we are watching the Peter Jackson *King Kong*. At the point where they reach the island and encounter the brown-toothed homicidal natives I open my mouth and say something I haven't planned on.

'Well, they clearly don't have a dentist.'

'Mum,' he says, 'Can you shut up?!'

And later on, watching Naomi Watts in satin evening dress dodging biplane fire at the top of the Empire State Building: 'She'd never have managed it in those heels.'

'For God's *sake!*'

He gives me a withering look before turning back to the screen. Here I am, enjoying watching one of my favourite films and interrupting with ridiculous, anachronistic observations in exactly the way my mother used to do.

Every week, when I was his age, we watched *Lost in Space*, about an average American family of scientists stranded on a remote planet forever trying to fix their spaceship and get back to Earth, with their friendly robot and a camp, waspish enemy agent whose role was usually to cause the trouble that constituted the plot. *Star Trek*, with its pseudo-philosophical observations on the nature of humanity, was another fixed point in our week. If in a certain mood, i.e. slightly bored, she would issue one of her observations.

'Well, I wonder where they're getting their sanitary towels up there,' was a favourite.

When it came to *Voyage to the Bottom of the Sea*, and the somewhat more masculine environment of a submarine, this would be modified into something like: 'What do they live on? You never see them have lunch.'

These inapposite remarks make her sound like one of those infuriating people who don't get the point of sci-fi but, instead of shoving off or shutting up, feel compelled to make supposedly amusing remarks all the way through to show how far above it they are. Or a certain kind of female who witters on through a film about the actors' hair, or what they're wearing, or in the case of one of my grandmothers while the family was watching a play by Harold Pinter: 'That's the sort of sofa I was thinking of for the living room.'

But my mother was the opposite of these. Despite the cracks about characters' sanitary arrangements, she was a genuine devotee of anything with space or monsters in it, and in my childhood always on the lookout for any classic, average or even frankly risible examples of the genre that popped up on television. What was so infectious about her enthusiasm was that she was as keen on such entertainment as *Attack of the Killer Tomatoes* as on the work of 'serious' practitioners such as Isaac Asimov and Ursula Le Guin. And she appreciated equally, each on their own terms, the three styles of sci-fi: unprovoked alien threats, such as *War of the Worlds*, monsters created or unleashed by man's foolishness such as *Frankenstein* and *Godzilla*, and the paranoid allegories of mind-control, like the anti-McCartyite *Invasion of the Body Snatchers*.

Peter thinks it's *really strange* for two girls to have grown up encouraged to rush through their homework so they could watch not very good actors being attacked by giant tarantulas or huge radioactive ants.

'What's strange about it?' I've said to him, somewhat impatiently, more than once. 'It's hardly as though I was the only eight-year-old who ever spent a sunny afternoon indoors with the blinds drawn, watching sailors fight off giant squid.'

'It's just so unusual. I mean, women are never into that stuff.'

'Well, I don't know what kind of women you've been hanging around with,' I say. Then I remember what he's told me about his own childhood. 'You're not just a teensy bit *envious*?'

'Well, no. But at weekends we did live in dread of being marched out on to the barren wastes of the Derbyshire moors.'

He grew up next door to the some of most beautiful landscape in England. He makes it sound like *The Bridge On the River Kwai*.

'It would have been nice to have watched TV a bit more,' he admits.

He sees it all as further proof of my marvellously bizarre upbringing. But he is right about one thing. A gorgeous-looking, well-dressed divorcee for a mother who invited you to stay up late every Sunday for *The Prisoner* was, I have to admit it, indisputably cool. And the fact that she knows *Blade Runner* is the film version of Philip K. Dick's *Do Androids Dream of Electric Sheep?* even more so.

Though I don't admit it to him, Peter has a point

about gender. As a male, and an even bigger film fan than my mother, my father should have been the one to get us hooked on flying saucers and oversized arachnids, but somehow the roles got reversed. He only ever took me to two sci-fi films: *20,000 Leagues Under the Sea* from Jules Verne's book about an underwater world run by a megalomaniac called Captain Nemo, which I loved, and the terminally dull 1936 'classic' *Things to Come*. Although he enjoyed James Mason battling a giant octopus and even signed some of his cards to me 'Captain Nemo', *Things to Come* confirmed his suspicion that the genre was dominated by men in silver jumpsuits intoning long, indigestible speeches about man's purpose in the universe. He should have blamed H. G. Wells, for writing an unfilmable book.

Sci-fi movies were B movies with good reason. Dad liked stars, and the genre was short on these. Steve McQueen was in *The Blob* in 1958 but he was unknown, and anyway the Blob took up most of the screen. The actors always played second fiddle to not just the monster but the idea. The first, 1956 version of *Invasion of the Body Snatchers*, is memorable for its terrifying depiction of humankind replaced by soulless alien replicas grown in pods, not who was in it.

My mother's quality was to be able to admire the restraint that racked up the fear in *Body Snatchers*, while also nursing a kind of irreverent reverence for its opposite: bad or inexperienced actors grappling not only with unworldly beasts and death rays but unsayable dialogue. An actor fleeing giant ants, a tarantula the size of a house or a swarm of killer bees and calling out – superfluously – 'They're headed this way!' or the line from the original *King Kong*, when the entire tribe stops the ceremony to stare murderously at the film crew, 'Too late: they've seen us!' genuinely gave her as much pleasure as any scene in *Casablanca*. And her favourite retort, when an actor picked up a phone during the action, was, 'He's calling his agent to say, "Get me out of this film!"'

The films I watch with Lawrence and Lydia are a direct result of my formative viewing years, although of course they have now become mainstream: *Men in Black*, *The Day After Tomorrow*, *The Matrix*, *Jurassic Park*, and *I, Robot* are to my children just normal films. They would be baffled to learn that sci-fi and fantasy were once the preserve of either bookish nerdy academic types who liked the high-falluting concepts, or – and I apologize if you were ever one of them – men who were single because they smelled.

My mother did for us what George Lucas was to do for everyone else a few years later, albeit on a slightly bigger scale: she liberated the treasure from these guys and gave it to the rest of us.

A couple of years ago I went to a talk given by Ray Harryhausen, the designer who created the fabulous spectacles among others of snake-haired Medusa in *Jason and the Argonauts* and the multi-armed, sword-wielding goddess Kali in *The Golden Voyage of Sinbad*. A pioneer from the days of stop-motion, he was scathing about television, which he denounced pretty much as mindless drivel. Everyone in the audience was roughly of my generation, so there could have been few, if any, who'd seen his films during their original release. At the end a few of us gathered round him for autographs or to say thanks.

'My mother brought me up watching your films on television,' I told him. It wasn't quite the compliment he wanted, but I needed to say it.

Recently I was leafing through a 1960s children's book called *The Book of Wonder* and I came across one of those illustrations of people in white zip-up jumpsuits that, when I was a child, represented The Future. One day, i.e. in the 1990s, we would all wear these things, eat nutrition pills for dinner and go to work in our individual spaceships. I was dreamily remembering this when automatically, without thinking, I heard a voice in my head say, 'White jumpsuits? Not for us women, I don't think, do you?'

26 There's No Such Thing as an – Ideologically – Free Lunch

September. After the summer holidays the diary fills up quickly. Saturdays fall prey to suppers with old friends, an Open Day for Lydia, a rugby match for Lawrence; best friends' birthday parties for them both. It's three weeks since our last visit and we don't have a clear weekend for another month. The year is slipping away and I realize we are in danger of leaving too long a gap. Too long for whom, though, I don't know; my mother never nags us, never leaves lonely little messages on the answerphone about the unpicked blackberries withering at the allotment. In fact, she never invites us as such at all. Instead, she'll ring to say that the farmers' market is on, or that there's a book sale in the village hall, events to appeal to mine and Peter's respective obsessions. But on her own desire to see us she is reticent.

For this lack of pressure I've always been grateful;

I've always felt so much freer than most of my friends. Even so, before I begin actually to miss her, after a month or so the normal bit of me, the bit that knows how often people should visit their mothers, activates my social awareness glands and they begin to secrete little drops of guilt. Like the people in the TV show *My Parents Are Aliens*, I pick up cues from the people around me which show how humans behave. And in keeping up appearances I can avoid thinking about what I really feel – or don't feel. Or at least I have avoided it so far.

When I am just beginning to wonder how long it would take for her to actually say she misses me, something very strange happens. I realize that I would really like to see her, possibly on my own for the day, and that the sensation is completely uncontaminated by guilt. And before I can get over the weirdness of *that*, the next evening she phones and asks me to come down for lunch. It's as if she's been on the same course, studying the humans as well. No, it's way weirder than that; it's as if we're in some bizarre way in tune. I get off the phone with her and feel happy.

'*Blimey*,' says Peter, who has to sit down to recover from the shock.

'I'm going to have lunch with her!' I repeat.

Twenty years ago, before I met Peter, I used to pop down all the time: just ring up on a Friday morning and be there in time for lunch. In summer we'd drink wine and eat her home-made chicken curry under the pergola.

Our favourite haunt for lunch in those days was the Christian café in Ashford. It was two doors down from the Odeon – possibly to counteract the decadent effect of the cinema – and run by people who'd apparently rejected the pulpit as too unsubtle and hoped to win converts instead through the more seductive medium of their cooking. It nearly worked. The service was slow, as if the servers were moving up the aisle with incense, but the soups and pies were delicious. In the staff and the atmosphere it owed something to the Women's Institute, making it wonderful value if, as my mother put it, you averted your eyes from the pamphlets. These were on the counter near the trays, so whenever we went in, we pantomimed holding our hands up as blinkers, to make sure any rays from the religious material didn't contaminate our thinking. We felt no guilt at infecting the premises with our atheism, however, and after a particularly good chicken and mushroom pie, my mother would announce, 'I do think, looking at the state of the world, that God would be better off sticking to catering, don't you?'

But God didn't do chips, so occasionally we defected to the Wimpy, which was ideologically even more problematic, as she had very didactic friends whose disapproval she feared, or at least pretended to. No meal there could begin without our hunching down in our seats, menus over our faces, in case any of them came past.

Though generally a healthy eater, she welcomed these lapses as she believed it was important to be inconsistent. She was suspicious of those with rigidly held beliefs, who were also invariably intolerant of imperfection in others, and saw them as a reason to avoid purity of any kind.

Her fondness for burgers was at least inspired if not actually provoked by her vegan friend Gudrun's succumbing in early middle age to cancer. Gudrun's previous avoidance of all culinary vice had been matched only by her keenness to identify the failings of others in that department. This made her some-what unpopular, confirming my mother's belief that our imperfections make us not only human, but tolerable. Gudrun survived, in my mother's view, not due to the diet of carrot juice she took up which was even more dire than her previous intake, but because she was too bossy to let the cancer take charge. Mum felt that the likes of Gudrun were apt to put people off what was otherwise a perfectly good range of food.

'There's nothing wrong with vegetarianism,' she told me once, 'except vegetarians.'

I check the trains and ring her back to make the arrangements.

'If we met in Ashford,' I begin, 'that would give us more choice, and there are more trains. So of course we'd have more time.'

Ashford is her nearest main station, a former market town ravaged by ring roads.

'Actually, I'd rather not if you don't mind,' she says. 'There are road works and I can't follow the diversion just now.'

'Just now' is one of the phrases she uses to suggest that a bit of habitual behaviour is only temporary. She's afraid of getting lost on the way to *Ashford*? I recognize her old phobia coming back, the fear of journeys and new places and things that might be unfamiliar. She used to go places, then stopped. And this was before she got old. Ashford, though. It's *four miles*.

Now her age has caught up with her outlook, her shrinking horizons are normal. Though I am frustrated by her fearfulness, I privately have some sympathy with it. As a teenager and twenty-something I felt I was supposed to go round the world with a backpack, or at least live abroad for a while, as most of my friends did, developing my character. But I hated travelling alone, never wanted to share a bathroom with strangers, and longed to be thirty so I would no longer feel like a freak.

I had the idea in my head that it would be a change of scene, get her out of her comfort zone. And we could laugh about whichever bit of the town they've ruined with their latest attempt to redesign the hopeless traffic layout. I can't cope with this. I decide to play the knee card.

'It's just that there are very few direct trains to your place and I don't fancy changing at Ashford if it means running up and down stairs to another platform.'

Though it's partly an excuse, I have confessed to an unwelcome aspect of my own deterioration, which is that I have bad knees. The left one is hurting more and more since I fell over five years back, and the thing that makes it twinge most is going up and down. Recently the right one has begun to hurt as well. *Is your journey really necessary?* I find myself thinking more and more often as I gaze upwards from the hall. With her tingly feet, something we now unexpectedly have in common is our dislike of stairs.

She does not dismiss my Knee Problem with a glib, *'Don't be silly! At your age?'* – a common and extremely irritating response of older people who seem to think they have a monopoly on infirmity. They're welcome to it.

'If you come here to the village I can collect you from the station,' she offers.

'God, no! It's only five minutes.'

'I mean, to save your knee.'

'Oh no, honestly. The walk is one of the high-lights.'

It really is a short and very pleasant walk, and anyway we don't do well in the car together. On our last trip on a country road she kept pulling over, half landing in the ditches, to let vehicles behind her overtake. I think she thought that by driving too close they'd make her panic and crash. The last time I drove her, she clutched the door whenever I went above twenty, and became so paralysed by anxiety she couldn't give directions to her friend Debbie's house, a place she'd been going to for years. Five minutes in the same vehicle is five minutes too long. Anyhow, the station is on a bridge and has no car park, so by the time she's pulled in, waited ten minutes for a gap in the traffic and turned round again, I could have walked it twice.

Also, since the Feet Problem she has taken to holding a walking stick in front of her – not to actually lean on but aloft, as if for the opening of Parliament. It seems to be made of some material that looks like wood but is of unprecedented density, so that wherever it goes it falls down all the time and when it goes in the car, invariably manages to get tangled up in something – the gears, the handbrake or the front passenger. This makes me want to snap it in two and hurl it into the river.

'I like walking through the village,' I say. 'I'll meet you at the pub.'

When I arrive she is already there and something of our old lunchtimes is in the air. She has been reading Richard Dawkins and brightens the autumn afternoon gloom by launching into a critique of his latest diatribe against the dark forces of religion. Despite this firmly held belief, she succeeds in wearing her atheism more lightly than I do.

No belief system, including that one, was pushed on us when we were growing up. I think she felt the whole idea of faith was evidently so absurd as to need no debunking. My father would look round nervously when any of us became too flippant about God, as if – like the Stasi – He kept mortals in line through constant surveillance. My mother regarded the whole thing as an essentially unthreatening fiction that could be imbibed in infancy without incurring permanent damage, like the Tooth Fairy or Father Christmas. It certainly didn't help – or possibly did – that my sister's primary school was run by High Church Anglicans, whose fondness for incense instilled in her an early association of churchgoing with nausea.

However, just because many of the worst things in history have been done by believers of one stripe or another doesn't mean my mother won't have one in the house. As she said when recommending the wonderful chap – a canon – who married us, 'He may be a bit of a Christian, but he's all right.'

We need to order. The pub's daytime gloominess cannot match the jollity of the Christian café. And the menu is disappointingly old-style pub, i.e. everything encased in breadcrumbs. But there are specials.

'Shall I read them out?'

They're on a distant blackboard which, with my new long-sightedness, I can read easily.

'Mushroom stroganoff, escalope of pork in pepper and cream sauce . . . I get to the end of a list of six.

'There's no vegetarian option.'

'Yes: mushroom stroganoff,' I repeat, a hint of impatience creeping into my voice.

'But stroganoff is a meat dish.'

'*Beef* stroganoff is. Mushroom stroganoff isn't.'

Now it's coming back to me why we haven't had lunch in a while.

'No. Stroganoff contains meat.'

'Stroganoff is the cream part,' I say. 'Hence the addition of the word "beef".'*

'You think so?'

She's doing that thing she does, looking at me with a faint smile, as if I have the intelligence of a beermat.

I know why we don't have lunch any more, because when we do, I want to stab her with a fork.

'Seeing as it contains mushrooms and not beef in this instance, would you like it for lunch?'

I try not to grind the word *lunch* too hard on my teeth. And this isn't the worst example. Once, years

* * *

* *Concise Oxford Dictionary*: 'stroganoff (of meat) cut into strips and cooked in sour-cream sauce (**beef Stroganoff**). *f* 19th C Russian diplomat.' Just so we can all move on with our lives.

ago, we were arguing about the difference between a food writer and a restaurant critic – because that's *so* important, isn't it? And somewhere in the middle of it all – I can't remember why – we got on to peanuts. I referred to them as 'nuts' – I was yelling at the top of my voice by now – and she finished the argument by saying, 'Actually, they are not true nuts at all, but *adventitious rootlets*.'

Peter loves that story. He wasn't there at the time.

I order another glass of wine.

'Would you like a drink?' I ask her. She is one of the very few people I know who is always improved by alcohol.

'I have one, thank you.'

She, who 'doesn't like sweet things', is on her second pineapple juice. At least it's consistent with her policy of inconsistency.

'I mean a glass of wine. To go with your food.'

'No thank you, dear.'

The food, beefless in both cases, isn't too bad. The conversation flows again, and after Dawkins we get on to another dubious quality we share.

'Listen to this,' I say. 'You'll like this.'

The week before, I have witnessed a low-level 'domestic' in a shop near where we live, with the unusual feature that the victim is a man. The shop is very narrow and the sound of the woman's slap on the man's face explodes right next to me. He doesn't react at all, but seeing that the perpetrator lacks tattoos or nose rings and is a good deal smaller than me, I tell her to stop at once, albeit sounding rather more like Miss Marple than I intend. And because I am moved by the presence of their small daughter, who is watching. Still, she stalks off, the man is grateful and I agree to give a statement to the police.

'A handsome young PC comes round,' I tell my mother. 'Really quite gorgeous. So of course I want the statement to take *ages*. But annoyingly I have to go out. Plus he's really bizarrely dressed, in a combat-material bomber jacket, you know, brown and green camouflage, and a yellow tie! "Plain clothes"? I don't *think* so.'

She is enjoying this.

'They don't type these things out – even back at the station. So he laboriously writes what I'm telling him, going *incredibly slow-ly*, and I start sort of explaining some of the words. I don't know what got into me, really. I was saying things like, "I saw the woman subsequently," and he couldn't spell it, so I spelled it for him, then I said – "It's Latin. You know, like 'sequence': when one thing follows another."'

My excuse is that Lawrence has recently started Latin and so it keeps popping into my mind, but I'm absurd, I know, and she hoots with laughter. Though we don't say it, there is a thin line between a stroganoff moment and this.

'I couldn't stop myself. He got me to read it, and it had these terrible mistakes, like *'she would of been about 30'*. Well, you can imagine! I just couldn't stop myself.'

'Oh no!'

'I'm thinking, if I'm asked to appear in court and they ask, *"Did you say this?"* I'm going to end up saying, *"No! I withdraw my statement on the basis that I would never ever have said that."*'

'Or never would *of*.'

'Hah! And the whole case will collapse.'

Without even trying, I have been in the outside world, miles away from her, behaving exactly like her. I even hear myself offering to come down to the station sometime and help any interested PCs with their spelling. That way I could show what a brilliant speller I am, and also, by hanging around the police station, pick up some more juicy nuggets. Whether she recognizes herself in this or not, she laughs again.

As we leave the pub and say goodbye, I decide we

must not let this lunch slip away, that next time we must recreate the conditions which have made it possible and remember the map of how we got here.

'We must do this again,' we say, and mean it as profoundly as two women parting after lunch ever have.

Her house is almost on the way to the station – a four-minute detour at my walking pace, but not for her.

'Let's go together,' I say, but she doesn't think it a good idea.

'I don't want to slow you down.'

We kiss lightly and say goodbye. Then I watch as she crosses the road, painfully slowly, leaving me on the other side.

27 Hip, Hip, Oh No

It is a month and a half since our pub lunch. One evening she rings me and says there is something medical she needs to tell me. Oh God. Unlike most of us – well, me – she never exaggerates anything to do with her health. In fact, she almost never rings about anything bad full stop, so this is obviously serious.

'I've been having a lot of pain in my hip,' she says.

'Phew.'

She's not dying.

'Sorry, dear?'

'I mean, oh. Go on.'

'Although it seems to have come on quite suddenly, it has actually been there for a while and has suddenly got worse. I've been to see Dr F, and he says I need a hip replacement.'

'Oh. Right.'

While I'm relieved she's not dying, I'm also

slightly disappointed it's not something more original. She doesn't conform to the norm in other
aspects of her life, so why should she in this?

'Well,' I say, 'I'm glad it's something mundane.
For your age, I mean. You don't want something the
doctors refer to as "intriguing".'

'No, quite!'

'And you *certainly* don't want something that
inspires them to rush out and call all the others in,
saying, "Hey, come and have a look at THIS!"'

'God, no!'

She sounds reasonably upbeat, if a little muted.

'So what happens next? When do they want to do
it?'

'I don't know. I want someone good.'

'Well, I could ask my knee man.'

'My knee man' is Mike W, who's going to put a
camera under my kneecap in four weeks, if I don't
bottle out. He's funny and charming and might have
a skilled colleague somewhere in Kent.

'You don't want to come to London?'

'Not really. No.'

'Well, we'll find someone good down there. I
imagine on the NHS there's a bloody long wait?'

'I don't know. I think I might want to go privately.'

'Sure!'

'That would be nice, thank you.'

Her local NHS hospital is famous, and not in a good way. I like the feeling this gives me, of being able to provide something so concrete. On the Day of Reckoning, when I get my inevitably bad daughter report, they will at least have to give me an A for providing. Well, maybe an A minus, since I told her she couldn't have a conservatory for her birthday.

'D'you think it's because of when you fell over getting out of the car?' I say.

'Oh, I don't think so, do you?'

She fell on to the pavement but didn't tell me for a week as she was 'fine'. Though I did worry once I found out about it, I still preferred finding out late to having the sort of parent who says, 'I burned my arm off while making a fragment of toast for supper, but I didn't want to bother you.'

So this is sudden, so sudden in fact that I go into shock. I know hip replacements are like wisdom teeth these days and everyone has them, just – not my mother.

'Peter's going away tomorrow but only for two nights,' I tell her. 'So I'll be down in three days.'

'Oh, that'd be lovely. No need to drop every-thing.'

'No. Yeah. Have you got painkillers?'

'Oh yes.'

'Hm. Well. I'll be there on Friday, OK?

I put down the phone and start trembling, and on the way to collect Lydia develop full-blown snivelling.

'I hope you didn't cry at the school gate,' says Peter at supper.

'Thanks for your compassion. Don't worry, I kept my umbrella down.'

At least it was actually raining.

'I could be there today if you weren't disappearing on *holiday*.'

He's going to Italy for three days with our friend Dom, who's bought a house there and needs help with his flatpacks. Taking things back to Ikea in Italy is even more fascinating than doing it here; Dom's vocabulary has doubled since he's returned several items and has had to hurriedly learn the Italian for 'This frame is not as described on the label', 'This is not the same length as *this*' and 'If you make me queue any longer, my family will report me as kidnapped'.

'If I hadn't already got my ticket . . .' he says.

'I know! Just fuck off and enjoy yourself. I'm sure she can wait in agony for three days.'

Until what? I arrive and release her from all suffering? Who am I, Jesus?

I ring Jan, her neighbour, and Debbie, her younger friend, to ask them to look in.

'With them around you don't have to worry,' says Peter.

'Yes I do.'

At 5.30 in the morning he goes off to Stansted.

'Be careful!'

'I will.'

'Look when you cross the road.'

'I will.'

'Remember they drive on the other side there.'

I must try to stop feeling so *terrified*.

After school I supervise the children's homework, a bit of the day I look forward to, as a smaller problem usually manages to take my mind off the bigger one. Today I'm doing fractions and lowest common denominators with Lawrence, which are ideal for fending off thoughts about death. Though I never would have said it at his age, I find maths – the bits I can do, obviously – rather reassuring. But every few minutes I have to interrupt myself to tell Lydia to stop drawing ponies and start labelling her plan of a Roman villa, and in the chinks between subjects my fears seep back in. I can feel them taking hold of me in the most terrible grip and I can't get back to feeling normal. I'm starting to behave like my father's aunt, who used to spend half a day worrying about whether to take the tranquillizers the doctor had prescribed to calm her down.

My mother has never been in trouble before, never scared me like this. When you think how most people go on about their ailments, we've been getting off incredibly lightly. I complain more about my knee in a week than she ever has about any part of her – ever. I feel the panic taking hold and spreading round my system like poison. This is worse than when I went to the doctor in tears with a lump in my breast which turned out to be an insect bite.

She's going to be in agony, then have a hip replacement, get MRSA and die. Or she's going to be in agony, have a hip replacement and never walk properly again. Or she'll die under the anaesthetic. Or they'll give her a replacement and she won't die but it'll be crap. Or the new hip will be OK but it won't matter because she can't walk properly anyway because of her tingly feet. Whatever happens, she is not ever going to be forty-five again. And one day, one day that is getting closer and closer and closer, I'm going to lose her.

And what I really can't handle is that I'm going

to lose not one but two mothers: the flawed one I've got and the perfect one I'm still seeking, because despite tons of professional help – I've had more therapy than Woody Allen – I refuse to accept things as they are.

Peter often says, 'Why don't you try and enjoy what you *do* get from her, instead of complaining about what you don't?'

And I reply to him, 'Why don't you try being a tiny bit supportive and listen to how the fuck I feel?'

It's like being married to the government.

'I find it helps to dwell on the positive,' he says.

'It's all right for you,' I say. 'Your parents are dead.'

What I really want to do is to get out of sight of the children and cry properly. But I stay in my seat, hoping that Lawrence's fractions will hold me together.

After a while Lydia says, 'Are you all right, Mummy?'

And I really don't want to lie to them. I've heard of loads of people who were really messed up by their parents' deceiving them about death or illness, pretending things were fine when they weren't. Well, one or two anyhow. Children know when there's something wrong and concealing it only unsettles them more. Besides, I'm rubbish at lying. On the other hand, you don't want to go down the route of the woman my mother knew who said, when the children asked if Daddy was going to die, 'Yes, quite possibly.'

'I'm OK, Lyd. I'm just feeling a bit sad for Granny because her hip is hurting. They're going to give her a new one, but – you know. It hurts.'

'I feel sorry for her.'

Lydia's capacity for compassion is limitless. I put it down to all that Circle Time, though one should bear in mind she has been known to feel sorry for a glove left on the stairs.

'Why don't you draw her a picture?'

'Can't you see I'm doing my HOMEWORK? Make up your mind!'

Well, OK: maybe not limitless.

On the third day Peter comes back from Rome and I go down to see her.

Things have changed. We can't go into Ashford as we used to and have a burger while marvelling at the latest mad incarnation of the ring road. We won't even be going to the pub in the village, as we did a mere six weeks ago. Instead we will laze at home with a takeaway and watch a bit of TV. In fact, we're going to be completely sleazy and have two takeaways, for lunch *and* dinner. The thought of this cheers us both up immensely, my mother because she loves both Indian and Chinese food, and me because we won't have to get involved with the oven.

But first I have to come in.

This time I find in the hall not just the big four-wheeled shopping trolley – this season's must-have accessory for the modern woman who wants less space in her house – but there's now a great big walking frame, also with four-wheels, as well. I move it pointlessly from one side of the hall to the other, so it leaves the same four-inch gap for me to squeeze through, except on the right instead of the left. Then I notice some new additions to the collection of things kept in the gap between the great big plan chest and the wall. As well as the broom, garden fork, rake and strange, abnormally heavy walking stick, I glimpse – no, it can't be: *ski poles*.

'They're fine. They've been lent to me by a friend.'

My mother will defend anything given or lent to her by a friend, no matter how bizarre. She's been given great piles of clothes in the wrong size, and brass coal tongs and shovels for a fireplace she does not have. She'd have a boat if one of them put it here. As for ski poles, have I mentioned that her village is not, as in *Heidi*, up an Alp? Nor is it even in Scotland, land of her birth. It is in Kent, and no more subject to snowfall than my home in London. But she thinks the poles will help. Even before her hip went wrong she's had more and more difficulty walking, because she can't feel her feet, and no one can tell her why. I'm furious with the medical profession for not being able to fix it, and furious with her for getting old. And now I'm furious because I can't get in the bloody door.

Eventually we reach the kitchen and have tea. She's not moving too badly, though I suspect she's on enough painkillers to stun a nightclub. Afterwards, she starts to get up.

'Why don't you have a lie on the sofa with the papers?'

'Well, yes, that would be nice. I just have to go to the chemist for my new painkillers. They said they'd get them in.'

'Have they got the prescription?'

'Yes.'

'Well, why don't I do it? That's why I'm here.'

She sinks slowly back down again, processing this unfamiliar idea.

'Oh, you're going to do that?' she says. 'Well, that would be very nice.'

'You might as well make the most of me.'

She frowns slightly, still weighing it up. This is someone offering to help her, with no ulterior motive, and she won't have to do anything back.

'Why not be lazy?' I say.

'Well, it does sound tempting . . .'

I give her another cup of tea and the Woody Allen book I've brought, and carefully lift her feet up on to the sofa. I'm always urging her to broaden her horizons, but now part of me wishes she could just stay here forever and not go anywhere she might come to harm.

I go to the chemist but they haven't unpacked their delivery yet. I notice for the first time that the shop is at the top of three enormous steps and wonder how anyone with walking difficulties can collect their prescriptions, or for that matter buy a razor or a tube of toothpaste. I go down the steps deliberately quickly so as not to seem as old as the other customers, my knees twingeing as I go.

I come back and start the job I've been really looking forward to: going through the paper on the kitchen table. The pile is about six inches high. There are letters about physio appointments, personal letters, including one from a very old boyfriend which I want to read but don't, bills – all paid, I'm glad to see, bank statements, catalogues of Old People products that I want to rip up and hurl on to a bonfire, leaflets about talks at the village hall and typed circulars of parish news. This is apart from all the stuff on the stairs. The stairs are her main in-tray.

'I'm just going out to get ring binders,' I say.

'OK!'

She's going to let me file them! I've been dreaming of this moment for years.

Oh, filing . . .

When I am filing, I can actually feel myself getting calmer. If I ever go properly mad, that, not pottery or basket weaving, will be my occupational therapy. It gives the illusion not just of order but of closure. If I punch holes in the letters from the hospital, the physio, the orthopaedic clinic and the neurologist, and put them away, I can pretend the problem with her feet has been solved. And if I file the bank statements I will relax and feel serene because they will no longer be on the table or on the stairs, in small random bundles held together with clothes pegs. And on top of that, if I am running in and out doing stuff, I am not sitting in front of her thinking about how mortal she is.

I come back and put the kettle on and we have a

brief exchange about the recent loss of twenty-five million people's bank details, downloaded unencrypted at the Inland Revenue on to two completely accessible CDs, posted to the National Audit Office and never seen again.

'It's terrible,' she says. 'Perhaps I should get a shredder.'

'I think right now that's the least of your worries,' I say, since (a) as a non-recipient of Child Benefit she doesn't have her details on the discs, and (b) in order to be shredded, the documents would first have to be removed from the stairs.

'Which reminds me, have you got a hole puncher?'

'Yes. It's up in the top room. It's a mess; don't look at it,' she adds, knowing that the top room is the zenith of inaccessibility, the sort of inner chamber that the ancient Egyptians should have used to protect their tombs, because any robbers trying to get in would have chipped away for ten hours then retreated in despair.

There are two top rooms, the first, larger one, and beyond that the tiny one, housing the photocopier, two cupboards full of antique prints from when she collected them and was going to sell them but never got round to it, another cupboard of assorted stationery and drawing materials and a filing cabinet of correspondence and document files, the latter mostly quite slim since the majority of the paperwork lives, as I say, on the kitchen surfaces and the stairs.

This lot would see anyone off, though I doubt whether they would ever get as far as the second room. Grave robbers entering the larger chamber and coming across this much unfiled paper would fall back and give up immediately. Put the gold sarcophagus behind the two hairdressers' trolleys full of used felt tips and you could pretty much guarantee your treasure would be safe. I go up to get the hole puncher and, feeling like Indiana Jones anticipating snakes, squeeze through the gap between the hairdressers' trolleys and into the inner chamber – where I behold the photocopier, cupboards full of antique prints, filing cabinet of correspondence and further document files, mostly quite slim, and – something I'd forgotten from my last trip up here, a dismantled baby's cot. I guiltily recognize the cot as Lawrence's, but concentrate on maintaining my focus on the object I must extract without bringing the whole lot down on top of me: the hole puncher. Finally I see it, in a half-closed drawer. I grab it and retreat past the dismantled baby's cot – dismantled baby sold separately – through the gap between the hairdressers' trolleys and down the stairs.

'Got it! Do you have a stapler?'

'Yes, of course. It's in the top room . . .'

I go back up and fight my way through the whole lot again for the stapler, the beautiful green and silver metal one I remember from my childhood. I love staplers; they hold things together. And this one is at least forty years old; we have nothing else from the same period still in perfect working order, and that includes me.

I take it to the newsagent's for refilling. On the way I imagine a stack of cardboard boxes of staples of every possible size, kept behind the counter and loaded into the individual staplers by men in brown coats such as ran the ironmonger's where my father used to get the paraffin for his heater. The newsagent's here is far more modern than that, yet with an appealing nod to the past: a dream shop combining the loving attention of a motherly owner with an infinite range of stock. In the event of Iran letting its bomb off, there'd be enough sweets, crisps, nuts, magazines, envelopes, DVDs, books of local history, birthday cake candles, jigsaw puzzles, Top Trumps and novelty keyrings to sustain the whole of Kent.

The motherly owner peers at the stapler and immediately identifies the size I need. Ahhh. I also see some dividers. I love dividers: Phone, Electricity, Council Tax, Gas . . . Mother, Daughter, Wife . . . Children, Mistress, Donor Child . . . They're just so definite, and so – male. In our family people constantly tell each other how to do everything – how to drive, how to cook, how to be a better person. The dividers can create an ideal world in which we all fulfil our own roles as opposed to everyone else's. I get three packs.

I come back, make another cup of tea and begin to divide my mother's life into categories.

I make two main piles: household bills and about forty bank statements in various states of crumpledness going back to 2003. Then, feeling deserving of a reward, I go out to get some wine. I put it in the fridge to chill, then I see it: the bag of pre-packed grated cheese. There can be only one reason why someone has pre-packed grated cheese in the fridge: because they cannot hold a piece of cheese firmly enough to grate it. This depresses me so much I slam the door shut and do a special Zen mind-clearing exercise – '*I am letting go of all desire to throw the pre-packed grated cheese out of the window.*' Then I put my head round the sitting-room door. My mother is still on the sofa, surrounded by books and magazines with half a mug of cold tea on one of the three small tables, the one she has painted herself with a leaf design. In other words, she is looking reassuringly the same as usual.

'I'm having great fun doing the filing,' I tell her.

'Thank you so much, dear. Did you remember the local paper?'

She has indeed asked me to get this, her favourite weekly read, not only for local news but for headlines like *School meals to face possible chop*. That one is still on my fridge, from when she sent it to me twenty years ago, and has been with us through three house moves.

'Bugger. My memory's shit, sorry.'

'Not if it's too much trouble.'

'No, no! I've got to go back for the prescription anyway.'

How can I forget one simple thing? I suddenly have a vision of us in ten years, her barely mobile, if still alive, and me wandering round the village for the third time that day wondering why I've come out.

I get the painkillers, noting that the repeat prescription has at least eight other items on it, and go back to the newsagent's for the paper. In the window there's an ad for a nearly new electric mobility scooter: 'Only £2,700'. You could get a second-hand Jag for that. On the way out I look at it again; does a second-hand scooter on the market mean someone has died? I suppose. I guess it's the adult equivalent of a star appearing in the sky every time a baby is born.

I come back, start boiling the kettle for another cup of tea and wonder, though it is only 4.45, if the wine is cold enough yet. I do some more filing and realize something shocking: she hasn't tried to stop me. She has even thanked me – for *filing*. Anything to do with the dreaded f-word, as with tidying, has always been the prelude to a bitter battle about order and chaos; she's always seen anyone who tidies, let alone *enjoys* it, as a proto-Nazi. The worst thing she can say about a person is that they're 'very efficient'. I once brought a friend for the weekend who washed up and wiped round the kitchen – as she'd been brought up to do – and Mum was furious. 'Very efficient,' she muttered at me as we left.

The terrifying thought occurs to me that she has undergone some kind of personality change. Is this the Beginning of the End? She is letting me file, so has given up on life. Oh shit. On the other hand, if she *has* gone a bit soft, this would be the ideal moment to get a new bin and kettle.

I've had my eye on this territory, the bit of the kitchen between the door and the cooker, ever since she moved in. Every time I open the door to the larder, where the bins are, the small, low-down bins with their bags that don't fit, I've cursed inwardly and, let's be frank, outwardly. And every time I struggle to wrench the lead out of the kettle so I can get it to the tap and fill it, I've vowed that one day I will make a cup of tea without dislocating my wrist. Now's my chance. She's in a good mood. Or she's losing the plot. Either way, I must seize the moment.

'I'm just going to get the kettle,' I say, as casually as I can. 'And, er, the bin . . .'

'OK, dear.'

I've got a green light. If this comes off it will mark the end of an era.

The village has its own hardware shop. They are helpful, though there is a weird, *League of Gentlemen* moment when I ask for a swing bin.

'A *swing bin!*' says the saleswoman, recoiling. 'We haven't had those for *years*.'

So I get one with a retractable lid, with which I return in triumph.

'I chose the smaller of the two bins they had,' I say. 'So it won't take up the whole cupboard. Just see if you get on with it.'

'No, that seems lovely.'

Lovely! I'll say. I've been building towards this moment for a long time. I pack the old kettle into the pyre I'm building outside the front door and text Peter of my victory.

'Congrats!' he texts back.

I go out and get crisps to eat with our wine. The evening passes in the most extraordinary way, with hardly any tension. Worn out by eight outings to the shops and all the filing, and to quit while I'm ahead, I go to bed at 9.30. I remember how it sounds when the people at the Chinese restaurant throw out their bottles, so I've brought my earplugs. It used to be a nice, quiet tearoom. I got my first ever job there, as a waitress, when I was fourteen. It's a measure of the difference between us that when it became a takeaway I moaned about the noise and my mother learned to say 'Hello' and 'Thank you' in Mandarin. Peter thinks this is the most wonderfully telling contrast in our attitudes to life, i.e. that I complain about everything all the time and she is a marvel and a saint.

I get seven hours' sleep, the most in a long time.

'I slept very well,' I say. 'How about you?'

'Fine.'

'I needed it too. Yesterday I woke up at four. I had the worst nightmare I've had for years.'

Although I know I shouldn't, I tell her about it. I ignore the sensible voice in my head saying, '*Don't tell her that. She'll make something of it*' – but I can't seem to stop myself. Every now and then I just have to offer up something she can get her teeth into.

I dreamed of an apocalyptic scenario, very like *The Day After Tomorrow*, which I have recently rewatched with Lawrence. What's stuck in my mind is the scene where Jake Gyllenhaal and his friend discover that the doors of the zoo have been smashed down by the ice and let out all the wolves. As in the film, we were holed up in a library, and outside there were wild animals trying to get in.

'There were these tigers,' I tell her. 'And every time more people came to hide in the library with us, they kept leaving the doors open. And I kept saying, "Shut the doors! The tigers will get in and eat the children!" It was terrifying.'

'Well,' she says. 'That one's easy to interpret.'

'Er, really . . . ?'

'Well, the wild beasts are your own aggression, threatening to harm the children.'

She delivers this in her neutral voice, the one she would use if she were a real shrink, instead of a fantasy one. I don't point out that the children in the dream were general, non-specific children, or that Peter was away that night, and I always feel anxious in charge of the kids at night on my own. Nor do I mention the timing, i.e. that I had the dream the night before this visit to see her, the first on my own for many years. Instead I say nothing, in the hope that it will seem like acquiescence so we can change the subject. She gets on to Jung.

'Jung had a dream about God once,' she adds, 'shitting on the world.'

'Oh. Right.'

As I look round the room in the attempt to somehow get away from this particular image, my eyes land on the chocolate truffles I've brought. They're not the typical round kind but a rather unusual shape. I gaze at them for a while, then suddenly realize what they remind me of: they're just like nipples. I mean, everyone's nipples are different, obviously, and no one's are generally covered in cocoa powder, at least probably not in this part of Kent. But these are exactly like those very firm ones, possibly as a result of extensive breast-feeding, that look a bit like rounded-off sandcastles. Then the thought comes into my head that hers may have been like that once, and I do a sort of mental stifle, in case she somehow knows what I'm thinking. Because I know that if she does know what I'm thinking, far from being shocked or horrified, she will say something like, 'It's interesting that just as we're discussing Jung, you're having a Kleinian wish-fulfilment fantasy.'

Melanie Klein was the one who – actually never mind. You'll just have to trust me on this.

It's been a good visit, but I'm about to ruin it. I have to get my train soon and I suddenly realize we haven't discussed Christmas. Maybe I should get a memory or two off her while I'm at it: fill in some of the gaps from her early life. It could also provide a sort of introduction to the subject.

'What were Christmases like when you were young?'

'Well, we had to spend it with the McPartlands, as you know, who were boring and awful.'

This is the only thing she has ever told me about Christmas when she was a child – I mean literally the only thing. They had to spend it with the people next door, whom they didn't like, and the husband was her father's boss at the bank, and his wife was incredibly stupid, and the husband was always impatient with her for being stupid. And Mum and her sister always watched the clock all day, itching to get home and play with their toys. One year my mother was so bored she drifted into the pantry and ate the whole remaining side of the turkey. The McPartlands blamed the maid and it was only when my grandmother mentioned that the girl was about to get the sack that my mother confessed. That's it: my mother's entire childhood experience of Christmas.

'So!' I say. 'If you want to come, which would be nice, Peter will drive down and get you.'

Now we are on our feet. She is facing away from me and doesn't turn round.

'Betty and I were agreeing we both find the whole family thing a bit much.'

Betty's one of her village friends. I bristle.

'What do you mean, "a bit much"?'

'The obligation, you know.'

'What obligation? There isn't any obligation. That may be a description of her family, it certainly isn't of ours.'

'Well, anyway . . .'

'That's incredibly unfair, can I just say, to lump our family together with hers. Is that what your friends think, that we're forcing you to come up to us? When we're not.'

'No, no, that's not what I said at all. You're so touchy!'

'But here I am, trying to tell you that Peter would drive down and get you, *if you wanted him to* – and you're telling people you're under an obligation.'

'If you'd just let me finish . . .'

'I just think that's so unfair.'

'Well, anyway. We've agreed to spend it together, having just the food we want and the wine we want, and then go home to our own beds.'

Even this last bit annoys me, implying that there's something wrong with our food and wine, when I know she really likes my cooking. But at that point I stop resisting, fold my arms and say, with just a teensy hint of bitterness, 'Fine.'

Buy your mother a Jo Bollocks scented candle from our festive range this Christmas: orange, vanilla and furniture polish with top notes of filial rage.

'I thought I'd told you.'

'No. Not a word.'

'Oh, maybe I told Claire.'

'Which is pointless, isn't it, because she doesn't even do Christmas.'

My sister, whom we are about to see for Chanukkah, has swapped one festival for the other. I have no desire whatsoever to try and bend her back to her former path, and rather like having a Jewish occasion to take the children to, but convince myself that my mother, who knows perfectly well which daughter does Christmas, has told her rather than me on purpose.

In my head all the crap starts swirling round. I can feel it building up, like a washing machine spinning faster and faster. Why does she treat family occasions as attempts to control her, and why does she never believe me or sound even a tiny bit pleased when I say we want her to come – but only if she wants to? Why *doesn't* she want to? This is the same person who, when I gave birth, went into rapturous speeches about the wonders of the Extended Family Group. When Lawrence and Lydia were both toddlers we heard a lot about the Extended Family, though nothing at all about Granny baby-sitting.

Peter's sister Jessica has remarried and her mother-in-law will be coming for Christmas and New Year from Glasgow. *And* she recently broke her leg. And she'll ask why Mum's not coming. And so will the children. I'm not even going to tell her that the children do really *want* her to be there. I can't bear the knowing smile I always get, the glib dismissal, as if to show me that she's not taken in by this trick.

Of course, they'll probably put it down to the hip – which she hasn't even mentioned.

Why couldn't you pretend you want to see us? If not me, then at least Peter and the children.

I can't do this.

I have to get out of here.

'OK, well, I have to get my train.'

Suddenly she flings open her freezer and offers me a chicken.

This sounds very Jewish – which she isn't, though it could be a subconscious tribute to my father, who sometimes used to turn up on my doorstep with presents of poultry and other non-gift-like food.

'I really need to defrost the freezer,' she says. 'I was wondering if you knew any tricks.'

'Such as not doing it when it's completely full? I've got to go now.'

'Well, yes, obviously. I just wondered, you know, if there are any tricks.'

'Start eating some of the food? Turn it off?'

'Well, I wanted you to have this.'

She makes the chicken sound like a bequest. It's from Woodpecker Farm, the most heavenly birds ever raised, fed and slaughtered. So I don't want to miss out. On the other hand, I'm in a hurry and it's a six-pounder. Blimey, she's got two in there. Well, that's OK then: I'm helping her empty the freezer, so it could potentially be defrosted in about fifty years, but not taking her last one.

'I love them, but I don't want to leave you chickenless.'

'No, no! I really meant these for you and the children.'

I put it in a bag I've brought with me, one of the ones she designed for her local farmers' market, with fruit and vegetables on the side.

'Just the thing!'

'Look, I can easily carry it.'

I pick it up and immediately feel my back hurt.

'Great!'

We hug quickly.

'Thanks so much for all your help.'

'I love filing, you know that.'

And I'm out.

Heady with my own boldness, I step out into the crisp afternoon air. The sky is still bright over the Downs and despite the awful exchange about Christmas I feel some optimism. Then I remember that however much filing I do, and however many knackered bits of household kit I replace, she is still going to get older and older and then die. This does not seem fair.

28 Don't Make a Special Trip

Two weeks ago I sat at this table punching holes in pieces of paper and putting them in ring binders, and feeling that I was bringing order to chaos. I put dividers in the ring binders and labels on the outside. I also did a lot of stapling, and, believe me, the stapler is underrated as a tool of therapeutic value. Every time she said something that irritated me, I leaned down on it particularly hard.

In less than three weeks she is going to have her right hip replaced. It's not a dangerous procedure; it's only a hip replacement, not euthanasia – though you never know: maybe they do a package. The hip replacement has been going for sixty years and is considered by the medical profession to be one of their success stories. But then they said that about childbirth. The fact that lots of people do something doesn't make it not frightening. Look at death.

Years ago I asked a very unanxious friend of mine if she was ever plagued by fears of losing the people closest to her. She looked across the kitchen at her husband and said, 'Of course. I often think he's going to die because I love him.'

I thought she put it very well. Isn't it why people in many cultures mutter a particular tiny prayer or make a sign to ward off the Evil Eye, when they say, for instance, how beautiful their children are? It seems to be normal, if not universal, to be afraid that our loved ones will come to harm, in particular because we've dared to have something wonderful. The gods might take us down a peg. My mother subscribes to a more psychological view.

'Fear of the outside world is fear of your own projected anger,' she would explain, observing that every single member of the agoraphobics group she belonged to was carrying around massive amounts of anger, though being agoraphobic obviously not carrying it very far. Certainly the women in the group, having been mostly beaten as children and ended up in unhappy marriages, had quite a lot to be angry about. The 'projected' part of it fell down, however, when one of them was arrested in the town centre for affray.

'Well, at least she's got over the agoraphobia,' said my father drily at the time. And my mother self-mockingly agreed.

'It must be the group, doing her all that good!'

She was big on 'unconscious anger', to which my father, going through his second divorce at the time, would say, 'I've got no unconscious anger against you. It's all conscious.'

It was while these financial wranglings were going on in court with my stepmother that he had his first heart attack – the low-level one the doctor called an 'episode', i.e. the type that scares the shit out of you without actually killing you.

He and I had recently had a huge row and I was leaving him to stew for a bit, so she called me to warn me.

'I just thought you should know that if he dies now you may find yourself crippled by guilt,' she said, more or less in those words.

The fact that he was not in hospital but ambling round Soho on his way to various appointments was beside the point. She just wanted me to know, in a helpful kind of way, that things *could* end really, really badly. And though I didn't want to hear it at the time, she was half right. He died ten years later of another heart attack, a much bigger one. By then we had come through most of our problems and had reached a sort of plateau. I felt no guilt about any previous anger, which like his was mainly conscious, i.e. the kind that leads to shouting in restaurants. So I had nothing to fear from his death. Nonetheless it was the worst thing that's ever happened to me, and I still feel cheated.

For quite a while afterwards, I thought that by paying the tax, doing the mountains of paperwork and jumping through the hoops, we could somehow win him back. Yes, his arteries were a bit furry but come on! They should have taken someone who'd done worse than get divorced twice and park on a few yellow lines.

My mother is beautiful, healthy and very interesting, in other words not the sort of person who's supposed to get old. People who get old are elderly-type people. She's stunning. Never mind that: she's never smoked, hardly drinks, doesn't have high blood pressure and doesn't wear old-lady clothes. Do you see what I mean? She's been wrongly filed. I know, because I've been putting everything in the correct folders. And she is in the wrong one.

DENIAL

ANGER

NEGOTIATION

ACCEPTANCE

These are the phases you're supposed to go through *after* a death. But me, I'm on stage 3 already and she's not even a little bit dead. That's what my father used to use as a generic euphemism for delivering bad news. You're supposed to build up to it in stages. There's a joke about someone being given advice on how to deliver bad news slowly so the person can get used to it, like say, 'A boy broke your window.' So, in order to prepare them, you say something like, 'There's a problem with your window . . . It's got a bit damaged.'

The guy's been given the advice but then he meets a man in the market who says he's got his neighbour's daughter pregnant. The neighbour will go berserk, so he needs to be brought round to the idea gradually. So the guy rushes home in a panic, sees the neighbour and blurts out, 'Your daughter – she's a little bit pregnant!'

So it became a family phrase. My mother still says it, which I like because it reminds me of when they were happily divorced and used to laugh at the same things. But then, she's not afraid of the word. Mind you, I used not to be, either.

When she joined Exit, years ago, we had a jolly chat about assisted suicide. We knew of someone who once helped another woman who was dying in terrible agony. The woman begged her for enough morphine to end it and so she gave it to her. But it wasn't enough. The woman was in a terrible state. So she put a pillow over her face. After she'd been in agony and had begged her to help her die. But she told someone she'd done it and ended up in prison.

'Maybe not the pillow then,' Mum would say, rolling her eyes.

'I could always hit you over the head with a mallet.'

Those were the days.

Our relationship is currently *so* complicated that even by the end of her life I may well not have made sense of it. I'll be like a scientist who spends thirty years studying the human brain, only to find she's mapped a mere 2 per cent. So, since I do love her but haven't even seen the plateau, let alone reached it, I should imagine that losing her is going to be a teensy bit of a blow. But then, using the deep insight bestowed on me as a student of the human animal, I reckon the death of your mother probably usually is.

I can't believe it. She is actually going to *die*. Maybe not today, as Humphrey Bogart said in *Casablanca*; maybe not tomorrow. But soon, and for the rest of my life. I can't think why I haven't realized this before. I think with getting married and having children and all, it must have slipped my mind. It's a bit of a shock to discover that even after your life is to a greater or lesser extent 'sorted', there are some pretty unpleasant things in store.

You'd think that after losing my father I would have got used to the idea. I know people don't last. They're full of design flaws and parts that go wrong, even without anything else unexpected happening to them. He wasn't even my first death.

His mother, my other grandmother, died when I was five and his sister the year after. Then there was my stepfather when I was eleven.

Lawrence got the hang of it at three, for God's sake, when Peter's aunty died. He said, 'Do people come alive again?'

And I said, 'Some people think so, but I don't.'

I was referring to a belief in the afterlife, though thinking about it now it sounds far more as though I was saying that some people believe in zombies. And Lydia has felt the pang of permanent absence for over two years now, since losing her favourite unicorn, Little Star, at the Science Museum. She designed a Wanted poster for her not long ago, which just goes to show that when love is true, death is emphatically not The End.

Nope, I still can't get my head round the enormity of it. So I'll do what I did when I was contemplating parenthood, what I do in the face of anything this terrifying: I will gather information. This will help me get a grip on the issue, or at least the *illusion* of a grip, as I can hear her saying, '*Get a grip on death? That's ridiculous!*' as soon as I even think it.

I don't mean information about death itself, obviously.

'What's death?'

'When you lose someone for good and they never come back.'

Yep, think I've got all the information I need on that.

The kind of information I'm thinking of is about the sort of funeral arrangements she wants. It won't change the future, but it at least does have, as well as being a distraction for me, the benefit of being something we do actually need to know. It's 'only' a practical thing and therefore won't have been a priority. She hasn't written it down, I know. The difficulty is choosing the right moment. And somehow I don't think once she's in hospital is it. Even if she didn't mind, I can envisage the nurses thinking, '*Bloody hell, that's not exactly subtle.*'

So right now is as good a time as any. I have to move quickly, because we're in one of our gaps between arguments and the mood can change at any time. Just when you're chatting nicely about books or films, the conversation can be derailed and even I don't plan on shouting – in the middle of a row – 'Burial or cremation, you fucking old witch!'

But before I get on to the vital subject, her friend Debbie arrives. Actually this is good. I have secretly emailed her to say I'll be there, as despite being much nearer my age she is one of my mother's best friends and a kind of emotional chaperone. Now that she's here, I feel it's safe to plunge in.

'There's never a good moment to talk about this,' I say.

'About what?' says my mother immediately, displaying her instinctive impatience with anyone who avoids a difficult subject even for a second, the conversational equivalent of those swimming teachers who, seeing you hesitate, have to push you in.

'There's never a good moment—'

'You've said that.'

Blimey.

'To talk about – well, your preferred, your – what sort of funeral you want. I mean, not *now*, obviously. But at some point. Because I don't know what you want.'

'Well, I quite like wickerwork.'

'Wickerwork's extremely expensive,' says Debbie. 'More than wood.'

'Well, cardboard then. I don't mind.'

'I'm going to have cardboard,' I say. 'And I've just been reading about coffins made from pineapple plants. Apparently after they harvest the pineapples they have to cut down the whole plant so there's a lot of waste. I think it's pineapple plants.'

'But what about the cost of getting them here? They're hardly native British species,' says my mother.

'Fair point.'

Now we've got going, moving on to the next bit doesn't seem so hard.

'I don't like cremations,' I say. 'They seem so much more devastating than burial, somehow.'

I can never watch the coffin moving off on its baggage conveyor belt. I'm about to say something about graves being a tiny bit less awful because you have something to focus on which feels more permanent, but then I remember that I never visit my father's because (a) it's miles away and (b) I don't feel he's there in any case.

'Cremation is very bad for the environment,' says Debbie, who as an environmental landscape planner does know which method of disposal will be least devastating to our surroundings, if not those left behind. 'You need to be buried,' she adds firmly.

But buried *where*? Then we must get on to writing down which music and poems she wants; she is very keen on poetry, including some really difficult stuff, so we might need to start practising pretty soon. But we never get to it. Somehow the conversation runs away in another direction and we end up talking about the funerals of Debbie's parents, or rather the behaviour of her family around them, and this is so awful and fascinating that I forget completely about writing down Mum's requests.

Then there are the hospital arrangements to talk about, and Debbie's generous offer to come and stay at the house for a bit. What with that, and all the stapling, the visit flies by and I have to leap to the train. So a few days later I phone her and revisit the subject, albeit from a diferent angle.

I tell my mother that Lydia and Lawrence sometimes ask us, 'How would you rather die? Would you rather burn to death or drown?'

She laughs.

'They go into quite a bit of detail as well; they're completely unsqueamish. Did we ever ask you that?'

'No, but you did ask from time to time, "Mummy, which of us do you love best?"'

'People always say they want to die in their sleep. Do you?'

'Oh, of course. Just wake up dead one day.'

'What would you like to be doing in your final moment? Certainly not "eating pâté de foie gras to the sound of trumpets" for me. I'd rather have steak and Miles Davis. Who said that, by the way?'

'The Reverend Sydney Smith.'

'You always know these things,' I say.

'John Wesley died, I think, singing hymns. He knew he was on his way out and it seemed a good opportunity, his family being ranged round, to give some of his brother's an airing.'

'Who was his brother again?'

'Charles. He wrote over 700 hymns.'

'Wow.'

'He was seemingly quite *joco* at the end. That's Scots for cheerful,' she adds.

Al Hirschfeld, an artist my father knew, said he'd like to go on drawing until the pen fell from his hand. I've just come across the CD of an interview Dad did with him when he was in his nineties, and notice how significant it is that I happen to end up listening to this stuff, recorded twenty years ago, the day before I have this conversation with my mother. On the other hand it is also the day Peter fixes the CD player.

'I have this picture of myself in a huge bed,' I tell her. 'With books and magazines and chocolates and cocktails – and a maid to bring them in on trays – surrounded by young male admirers who'll come and sit on the bed and flirt.'

'Lovely!' she says.

'What young men?' says Peter, giving me one of his looks.

'Shut up. I'm on the phone.'

'Another of your sad fantasies,' he mutters, shaking his head.

Bill Deedes has recently died and I've been renewing my interest in him as a role model. It's probably a bit late for me to cover the 1937 war in Abyssinia, edit the *Daily Telegraph* and become a Cabinet minister, but I might manage to spend my last months sitting in bed in a nice house in Kent with a glass of Scotch and a laptop, gazing out at the orchard and the chickens. I'm about to put this thought to my mother when she says she has to go. So I send her a questionnaire:

17 Dec 2007

Dear M

In lieu of an immediate visit, and because I didn't get round to all this on Saturday here's a mini quiz:

- *People always say they want to die in their sleep. But if not that, what would you most like to be doing?*
- *Anything you wish you'd done in your life? Not done?*
- *What would you* least *like to be doing in your final moments?*
- *Which historical figure would you most like to have met? What is your*
  Best quality?
  Biggest fault?
  Favourite book?
  Desert Island *piece of music?*

My other reason for doing this, of course, is that I'm thinking about it for myself. I've got a document in the computer I've been tinkering with for about five years that still isn't finished. For a start I'm too indecisive. In fact, on that theme of what you'd most like to be doing at the end, I can quite imagine myself printing it out, but still changing the songs, speakers and so on right up to the last minute. My last words will probably be, 'Can I have that back a second? I just want to change one thing.'

Actually, as an epitaph it would almost do.

Also, I do think quizzes are a good way of handling, i.e. avoiding, impossible issues. The questions I enjoy most are about the things you wish you had or hadn't done. Woody Allen, when asked if he'd have done anything differently in his life, answered, 'If I had to live my life again I'd do everything the same, except I wouldn't see *The Magus*.'

Later, when she's out of hospital, I find this scribbled on sheets torn from a lined pad, sitting on her kitchen table, apparently awaiting my attention:

> For myself, I think on the allotment would do fine when I'm 'fetched'. A favourite story tells of a very old man working on his garden when a little boy approaches him, smiling.
>
> 'I've come for you,' he says. 'It's time.'
>
> And the old man says, 'Just let me finish planting this row.'
>
> But the child takes his hand firmly.

'You have to come now.'

And why should Death always be a scythe-wielding hoodie anyway?

I take this home and read it in bed – not, as planned, on the train – which is just as well, because it makes me cry.

I would like to have done microbiology, as well as, not instead of, all the drawing/writing.

I would like to have done graphic novels (only recently invented today).

I don't regret the affairs I've had.

I do, though, Mother! I can't help wishing that someone of her beauty and intelligence hadn't invested so much time in seeking validation from the attention of men who were either dull or selfish or both. The interesting and brilliant ones – well, my father – were impossible, and my stepfather died before he could really prove himself. I read on:

I seriously regret that neither of you thinks I was a good mother to you but you have both been the joy of my life and if I never said it I'm saying it now.

Whooah. I have never said the former and she has not, I think, expressed the latter. Or not so we could hear. With very few exceptions, I don't believe you can divide people into 'good' parents or 'bad', and I think that our relationship is testament to that.

I'd like to be cremated (just check I'm dead first). There's a James Bond movie where he's shoved into a coffin, and finds it's moving into the incinerator and it gets very hot as he struggles to undo the screws on the lid before he is crisped.

I should like a green burial: cardboard coffin etc. A humanist-type memorial service, possibly in the village hall. Nice music. Kodály, Bartók, Stravinsky, Ravel's 'Pavane for a Dead Infanta' or a good choir singing bits of St Matthew Passion. A recording of Hebridean 'mouth-music' as practised by poor island folk with no musical instruments would be great.

Fave books: Russell Hoban's *Riddley Walker*, or poems by Gerard Manley Hopkins or Wallace Stevens.

I would rather not die siting on the loo like Elvis but apparently it's not uncommon. Scatter my ashes anywhere in the Western Isles (don't make a special trip!).

It's this last bit, 'don't make a special trip', that tells you it's written by a woman.

Thinking this over, I remember something my friend Geoffrey once told me, an extraordinary idea of his late wife's, Carolyn, about her preferred way to depart the mortal coil. Thirty years ago Geoffrey was my Latin teacher. I've learned quite a few things from him over the years, most of them outside the classroom.

'Did you once tell me,' I ask him, 'that Carolyn had the idea of getting hold of some supermarket trolleys, going up a hill somewhere in the Lake District, drinking lots of champagne, getting in the trolleys and launching yourselves off the top?'

He laughs.

'Did she really say this, or did I dream it?'

'No, indeed!' he confirms. 'Like a toboggan going over the 2,000-foot vertical drop – and ending up a mangled nobody at the bottom.'

'I like it.'

'Yes,' he says.

'Was there an exact spot?'

'Very much so. They're called the Wastwater

Screes. Actually we went up there this year with some champagne and scattered her ashes.'

A few days later I get some photocopied pages of Wainwright from him in the post, with an arrow showing the proposed ascent of the trolleys, and the actual route of the champagne party, up Whin Rigg, ending in a little blue 'x'. And I think what an extraordinary creature the human being is, that for all the brilliance of aeroplanes and epidurals and tin openers and MRI scans and the Internet, there is nothing to match the wonderful, quirky beauty of how people express themselves to each other. And that despite our medical and technical wizardry we still cannot protect the vast majority from dying horrible, undignified deaths. Carolyn died, not flying over a rock in the Lake District, but of ovarian cancer in a hospice. That's about how much control most of us have over our mode of exit, i.e. none.

Jesus.

To avoid leaving you *too* depressed, here is a nice memory of Kath, a woman I knew who died, in her forties, a few years ago. We shared a childminder and her son, Roman, was Lawrence's first friend. The last time I saw her, I went over to her house to find her making a list of favourite tracks with a friend for the friend's forthcoming birthday party. Kath was deeply into doing this list, and unbeknownst to me had a great collection of original singles on classic labels like Motown. Suddenly she jumped up, shoved back her chair and said, 'Come on, let's have a dance!'

She bunged on the singles – she had kept her old record player – and the three of us danced round the room to the Supremes' 'Stop! In the Name of Love'. Lawrence and Roman were playing with Roman's Lego at the time, and much to their frustration we danced over and around them and their carefully constructed towers. Two months later she was dead. When I feel despondent about life, and the losing of it, I remember this and am reminded of what a miracle it is that, for this meaningless little fragment of time, we are here, and meet each other.

29 I Am Not Becoming Her 5: The Houmous Pots Are Massing

For years I thought of myself as the offspring of a single parent: my father. I shared his taste in music, food and films, and had the same, almost religious devotion to tea shops. Whenever I found myself in a new place I'd seek out a venue with a cakestand in the window, much as some people look for a golf club or church. Added to the hairy legs, flat feet and bipolar tendencies, it pretty much identified me as the product of twenty-three chromosomes not forty-six.

Or so I thought. I was well into adulthood before I realized I am my mother's daughter, though not quite in the way I would have liked. I don't have her tall, slim figure, nor her gifts for drawing or poetry. I lack the prodigious memory, appreciation of nature and understanding of literature and art. But I am unable to throw things away.

In the future, science may develop to the point where people will be able to identify embryos with the gene for messiness and, if not abort them, at least prepare them for a life blighted by piles of old newspapers and leaning towers of Tupperware. But for me, it is too late. When I visit her and we eat dinner in the gap between the used envelopes and the old parish magazines, I see my own future and shudder. Sure, I grab the piles and carry them, cursing, into the hall. But she doesn't know the shameful truth, that I have piles on my table too.

Did my grandmother have the gene? Sadly yes. Even by the standards of her generation, whose daily prayer was 'Waste not, Want not', she was unusual. Her larder, which we used to hide in, contained enough jars, packets and tins to sustain a small town. If Hitler had attempted his invasion they could have lasted out the war in there, emerging for the armistice in fine health, if a bit high on sugar due to the preponderance of cling peaches. Behind the white metal cupboard doors in her state-of-the-art 1932 fitted kitchen, she preserved ancient monosodium glutamate and many other antique packets, riveted by age to the larder shelves, along with decades of coupons – 'Send 12 sardine tin labels and 5/- for one silver-look cake slice', until they were long out of date, and the companies which issued them had closed down. She was always smartly turned out as a rule, and was never seen outside the house without one of her matching dress and jacket ensembles, adorned with the marquesite peacock brooch and, if going to the theatre or a bridge game, her fur stole as well. Yet inside her wardrobe were boxes and boxes of new stockings, while she wore the same two pairs into holes. And even as I am having this thought I know that I recently went to a wedding in tights I had carefully stitched up the night before.

'One of these days I'll definitely wear one of the new pairs,' I promise myself, but no occasion ever seems quite special enough.

My sister thinks she has the gene too, though unlike me she is not trying to hide it. I know these things are relative, but she is way tidier than me, with only two piles on her kitchen counter and stair clutter which is smarter than mine. For example, her landing does not feature a large, not particularly attractive stone taken from New Romney beach – not so much the Japanese look as the 'What the hell's that doing there?' look.

'I have lots of crap,' she insists, 'including a voucher I've had for a year to get £1 off a magazine

I don't even like.' She also claims to have an entire room in her house which is 'full'.

'Of what?'

'I don't know. We can't open the door.'

It's all relative, of course. We're already deemed peculiar because our children spend weekends playing computer games in their underwear instead of having violin lessons or upping their batting average. And my sister seems more slut-like because she lives in the tidiest neighbourhood in London.

'Round here I'm regarded as a total sleazebag because I dry my pants on the Aga.'

She has a point. At seventy-nine my mother is one of the younger people in her village, so it's unlikely the neighbours are going to come round and sneer at her cloths. In any case, the ones who can still get themselves there may well have no sense of smell.

Whereas I blame her for it all, my sister reminds me that we are the issue of *two* hoarders, which genetically is as bad as cousins.

'People similarly afflicted should never breed,' she says. 'The problem is magnified horribly, like the Habsburg chin.'

Naturally, I took care to avoid my parents' mistake when choosing a mate. I rejected one prospect whose flat was full of transport memorabilia, old magazines and cats, complete with smelly tray in the kitchen. Another's was engulfed by records. But when I met Peter I knew I'd got it right. His flat was neat and clean, with no shelves full of every *Star Trek* episode ever made, Airfix models in progress, or anything else suggesting he was thirty-five and single for a reason. The downside was that, tidiness-wise, he was able to grab the moral high ground and stay up there for the entire marriage.

He says, 'Of course it annoys you in your mother. You do a lot of the same things.'

We've been together for nineteen years, which shows I've put up with a lot.

'I can't believe you said that. That's such a lie!'

My mother isn't too bad on tights – she has about 200 pairs, all out in circulation and none saved for best – but she does keep several bits of nearly fin-ished soap round the bath and the basin at all times, which I never do. The comics of her youth – and mine – used to tell you how to melt the pieces in a pan to make one decent-sized, multi-scented bar. But these just sit there.

'And what about the dreadful cloths round the sink? I'm nothing like her, you arse.'

'What? My whole aim in life is to try and clear all the unnecessary things out of the marriage, while you constantly try to thwart me by dragging them back in.'

He gestures at the kitchen counter.

'A Calman pile,' he intones despondently. 'You think it's just paper, but when you lift the top layer, you find, in between all the newspapers and brochures, a tile, a drawer handle, some curtain fabric, several shopping lists and always, for some reason, a glassless picture frame. My mistake,' he says, 'was to believe I could pull you up to my level. But no, you've dragged me down.'

Sometimes he is startled by a yelp as he swings the hall closet door shut, only to find he has almost tipped me into the paper recycling box, whose contents I'm studying. Perhaps there's a scientific paper to be written on why the articles in magazines that have been thrown away or used to soak up washing-machine floods are so much more fascinating than the ones on the table in front of you. Or more to the point, one on why men marry women with the very habits that annoy them. I mean, whose fault is that?

'What about this?' he says, holding up a quarter-lemon pulled from the fridge. He is confident enough to know that he can swing open the door and find something to prove his point. Except he's wrong.

'It's a piece of lemon! And – crucial detail – not mouldy. See?'

I grab the lemon, wave it in his face and shove it back.

'So bugger off.'

'And ha! What's *this*?'

He has opened the drawer underneath the kitchen counter, where we keep the foil and so on, and is brandishing a small piece of cling film.

'It's the rest of the bit I tore off, for when I put away the rest of the lemon. What's so bloody weird about that?'

'You are sweet,' he says, laughing, which annoys me even more. I accept a hug, but only for long enough to reach behind him and manoeuvre out of sight an empty gold chocolate box I'm keeping for Christmas to cut up into gift tags.

'Just leave me alone,' I say, as I push him away.

I am nothing like my mother. She doesn't put things away but keeps them arrayed all over every surface, as if permanently hosting a jumble sale. The drawers of the plan chest in her hall are even kept slightly open, as if part of a display. They used to have to be that way because several of the handles had come off and so if they were ever shut couldn't be opened again, but even after I'd solved that problem by getting new handles – which Peter put on – they remained open, as if in tribute to the original, departed handles. But that's not the reason. The drawers are kept permanently open because if she shuts them she won't remember what's in them. I know, because I am starting to do the same.

Once I've put things away – not all things, only certain things – their existence is unknown to me. It's how I forgot I had a winter coat. It's how I ended up buying an unnecessary £20 attachment to plug the memory card from the camera into the computer; we already had the lead connecting the two but it had been put away in a drawer. Eventually I found it, and even then I had no memory of why it was not in the camera drawer but in the chest where I keep my stationery. I have been known to buy the same jumper twice because of this, and the same CD.

'You made me put the CDs away,' I explained to Peter on that occasion, 'so it's your fault.'

And I'm not telling my mother. But I'm rattled enough to do a bit of cursory tidying on the spot to head off any suspicion he might have that it is getting to be a habit. Because I know he is secretly trying to drive me insane. Like the bloke in *Gaslight*, he is trying to convince me of a false reality, but whereas the husband in that turns the lights down and tells his wife she's imagining it, mine compares me with someone who keeps a pile of ponging cloths by the sink. And when that doesn't work he tries another tack.

'The houmous pots are massing again,' he says, thinking that because he's making them sound like the rooks in Hitchcock's *The Birds* I'll find his observation fresh and charming instead of predictable and annoying.

'I'm keeping *four*,' I say. 'For the children's snacks. In fact, you know what? Throw them away. Throw everything away. Will that make you happy?'

Because he has no parents, I've got nothing to get him back with.

Or wait. Have I?

He always presents himself as this lean, ascetic type whose landscape has been blighted by me and my *stuff*, whereas this is a load of spin.

When we first met, yes, his flat was tidy, *but* he had boxes of model cars under the stairs, cat litter trays in the kitchen and – and yes I did sleep with him after I'd seen it – the front half of the bonnet of a 1938 Chrysler in the fireplace. So *ha*.

Whether he'd got this from his parents, it was hard to tell. They both died before we met. However, the family home in Sheffield was still occupied by his stepmother and only came to be sold a few years ago. I'd met the stepmother: spent a weekend there early on in the relationship on a visit when we ate our own weight in saturated fat, leading me to wonder if she was trying to get the house by inducing heart failure in the other beneficiaries. In turn I made an impression by leaving a pair of my pants in the bed. They arrived subsequently in the post, cleaned and ironed, though without a note.

Other than that I remember admiring the tidy rows of jars in the larder, and the way his father had kept all his nails and screws in the garage in neatly labelled Old Holborn tins, and his tools hung up on special pegs. God, it was beautiful.

But his parents had a dark secret in the attic. When their stepmother died he went up with his sister Jessica and they filled *sixty bin bags*. The majority of this was blamed on the stepmother and in particular her knick-knacks from around the Commonwealth and an unbelievable quantity of Pyrex cookware. But the attic went back to his parents. When Peter hedged and changed the subject I made his sister tell me what they found there, and eventually, she did: two photographic enlargers, three bedheads, a bench, a fireguard, the stair runner from the previous house – which they left in 1955 – their father's trunks from university and the army, their mother's from teacher training college, a toy chest, a never-assembled wine rack, eight suitcases – one full of used envelopes – two folding beds, a Camping Gaz stove, four tents, 150 school textbooks and enough underlay to cover France.

'So!' I say. 'You can stop picking on *me*.'

'I don't pick on you,' he says. 'Just point out from time to time that some of your piles are like your mother's.'

'D'you want to stay married?' I ask him. 'Or what?'

At bedtime we go up to kiss the children. And I notice something disturbing, more disturbing even than any – perceived – similarity between myself and my mother, which, as I say, is in Peter's head.

Whereas Lawrence is lying under his duvet, with just a spare book, a teddy, a pair of jeans, a fleece and a T-shirt discarded on the end of the bed, Lydia is buried as if under an avalanche. Around and on top of her we can see three books, a diary, a notebook, two pens, a unicorn, a polar bear, a kitten in a basket, a pair of jeans, a top, her school swimming costume and some knitting. And we're still only in the doorway. Closer inspection reveals a purse with 20p in it, a bit of felt with a needle sticking out of it and some doll's house dolls sitting in chairs, all ranged along the gap between the headboard and the pillow, like tenants stuck in a bad flat conversion. It is, if you swapped the toys for books, clothes and newspapers, an exact replica of my mother's sleeping arrangements.

It's not as though I've never noticed it before, but I hadn't realized the significance.

'It goes down the female line,' says Peter, with what he appears to think is a twinkle in his eye.

I kiss my sleeping daughter and go to bed with a book.

Soon after this I am putting some things in a bag to take to the charity shop. I have a few unwanted household bits, and both children agree to relinquish a few toys, which in Lydia's case represents about 0.01 per cent of the stuff on her bed alone.

'Still,' I tell Peter, 'it's better than nothing.'

'Well done,' he says. 'By 2050 we should have the room clear.'

I use the same technique as when we got rid of my mother's old boyfriends' shirts and bedlinen, taking things away to 'give to someone we know who'd really like them', and then spiriting them off to the dump. This way I manage to persuade Lydia to part with two semi-naked dolls who've been scribbled on – 'some other child would love these!' – and a hideous plastic teaset.

I leave the bags by the front door. That night when we come in to kiss her, we find that she has sneaked all her stuff back – not only the plastic teaset and defaced, naked dolls, but also *a pair of shelf brackets* that were in the same bag. The shelf brackets weren't even ours, but were put up by the people who owned the house before us, so badly that they fell down. They have been awaiting removal for six years.

As we go back downstairs I remember my mother and the tomatoes. On one of our visits to my grandparents', she found some tomatoes, mouldy, in the fridge. She showed them to my grandmother and told her she was putting them in the bin. When we came back that afternoon, she'd got them out and put them back.

'Drink?' says Peter.

'Yeah,' I say. 'A large one.'

My mother saw this in her own mother, but does not see it in herself. Am I similarly blind? She puts face cream on and doesn't smooth it in. Will I do that one day? Open the door to Lydia with moisturizer on my face and *refuse to wipe it off*? Even shuffle down to the shops with it still there, and a horrified Lydia running after me with a tissue, begging me to turn back?

And will I keep saying, 'It's fine actually,' as she storms back to her car, vowing never to come again?

And will she and her daughter be the same?

This is too dire a prospect to contemplate. I will *have* to listen to Peter, because if I don't I will end up like the spaceship *Nostromo* in *Alien*, sailing along as if everything is normal when there's a dreadful clawed thing whipping around in there, destroying all in its path. The crew will go down one by one, and it won't be long before *It* is entirely in control. If that happens, Lawrence and Lydia should board their shuttle and get as far away as possible, sealing the door and leaving me closed in, with my lemon quarters and my empty chocolate boxes and my houmous pots, whirling alone in space.

30 How Do You Know I Love You?

December. A week before Christmas my mother phones me in tears.

She's had a scene with my sister who has accused her of not showing enough interest in the three grandchildren. Peter hands me the phone and I want to run away. Half of me thinks, *Oh, shit: my mother crying*. And the other half thinks, *Great! My chance to be the Good Daughter*. I can say, 'There there, mean old Claire', and she will love me more. Except Claire and I always stick by each other, and anyway I think she has a point.

On the other hand, I really must seize this opportunity to try and see both sides in a Peterish way, be all calm and mature and understanding, and come out praised by both of them. Yeah, that's what I'll do! The odds against my managing it are so long that I can't even see where they end, but I attempt it anyway. Well, I make an attempt at an attempt.

First, I acknowledge that my sister's expectations

are fairly high, higher than mine anyway, and that she is now part of the Jewish community, which prizes family involvement above all. So the goalposts may have been ever so slightly nudged. But then I start defending her position, partly out of the instinctive loyalty which has kept us as close as twins for over forty years, and partly because, as I say, I think she has a point.

'I think you should let her know that you do love them,' I say. 'Mine and hers.'

'Well, of course I do!'

What should happen now is that I express the views of both sides and bring them closer together. But when I hear her amazement and outrage, I think, *But this is your doing, you old bat! You read the paper instead of playing with them. What do you expect?* I'm as feminist as the next man, but I blame all that women's-group assertion training that taught her how to say No. I was right behind it until I realized we were the only people she ever learned to say it to.

But still, I have this opportunity to be if not the Good Daughter, the Slightly Less Bad One – at least this week.

'The thing is,' I say, 'I don't doubt you do love them. But maybe the message just isn't getting across.'

And I'm beginning to think I know why. My sister has her rules about how you express love, concern, closeness; I have mine. We all do. What you hope for is to meet someone who has the same ones. I *know* Peter loves me, but if he didn't give me a birthday present one year I'd be inclined to whack him across the head with a pan. Every year millions of women eagerly await their Valentine's Day presents and millions of men don't come up to scratch. The two sexes have such different rules about the outward display of feelings that the whole concept is set up to fail. St Valentine: God of Disappointment. My mother doesn't participate in family life but sends hand-drawn cards which are often beautiful and to her probably represent the strongest expression of affection but to us are no substitute for a visit to school Open Day or a 'Well done!' after a race. The children love her, and I don't doubt that she loves them, but the connection doesn't feel 'live'. It's my problem, Peter would say, because of my high expectations. And I have to admit he has a point too. Who's to say what's the right level? If we all had the same – 'right' – expectations, no one would ever divorce.

'Everyone's different,' I say, reattempting the Key

Stage One mediation. 'Some people just need more expression of it than others.'

Wow. That's me sounding really diplomatic, i.e. not like me at all. I hope that saying this will switch the train on to a different line, to a more civilized destination. It's the sort of thing the books tell you to say, that will elicit a positive response. But she just snaps, 'Evidently!'

And somewhere in the back of my mind is the other reason for the gulf between our ideas of what's 'normal', the fact that my children are growing up in a time when physical affection has sprung out into the open. When I was young, for instance, you never saw a man pushing a pram. My father was demonstrative because he had suffered such terrible separation from his parents during the war, but he was very unusual. And it wasn't just men; individual parents cuddled their children of course, but the general atmosphere was far more restrained. The books I learned to read on showed Peter and Jane sailing their toy boat or building sandcastles and mother and father engaged in their prescribed roles – father behind the wheel, mother naturally at the sink. There was no physical contact shown between adults and children. Now children's books are about hugs and it being OK to be scared of the dark and show kids sitting on their parents' laps or being thrown playfully in the air. There's been a revolution. The first time I got one of many report slips saying that my adventurous daughter had scraped her knee or been run over by a trike in the playground, the teacher had written 'Gave plaster and TLC'. In my day, if you got banged or bashed at school you were lucky to be left alone. Crying was likely to provoke a slap on the head.

I've had my children in very different times. Now nine and ten, they fall into our arms and say, 'I love you!' at least once a day. Lydia even calls it out to me at the school gate and we mouth it to each other secretly sometimes when we're out. And always mouth back 'I love you too'. I may criticize the maudlin outpourings unleashed by the death of Diana, but otherwise I like living in soppy times. It's a joy to have children who pull you down to tuck them in at night and cover your face with kisses. It was not, of course, the experience of my mother's generation. Where she learned to cuddle us I don't know, but she did. Still, the gulf between our expectations for the grandchildren yawns open.

So maybe it's partly because of this endlessly affirming era that we live in that I want her to sing the children's praises more and, most of all, to express the desire to see them. She may not be able to right now, but I want her to *want* to. A career in mediation is not, I fear, within my grasp.

'I think,' I say firmly, 'we need to hear from you that you're interested in them.'

'Oh, well, whatever I do, it'll never be enough.'

'No. It will be. We just need more than a few cards.'

'Cards made by *me*!!'

This reference to her art is the angriest she gets during the whole conversation, practically spitting.

'OK, *made by you*. It's not enough. I mean, how would you feel?'

I have no arguing skills. The whole thing's slipping away from me.

'I wouldn't feel anything. I don't judge other people's behaviour, you see.'

'Really?' I say. 'That's unique.'

I am gripping the phone really tightly now.

'And,' I say, 'I think we'd all like to hear a bit less about other people's children. That would help too.'

'Other people's children? What do you mean?'

Even on the phone I can see her peering down at me from behind her white coat, straitjacket at the ready.

'That boy you're always on about.'

I want Lawrence and Lydia and Leo to be her favourites, not the truanting eight-year-old from Dover, her latest project. Since her intervention he has joined a swimming club and won a race, a triumph I get to hear about on every visit. Lawrence's big achievement this term, a certificate for twenty-five house points, she forgets as soon as I've told her – twice. If I met this boy I might well feel just as much sympathy as she does; instead I feel only jealousy and rage. She has never seen my children run a race, never looked round their classrooms, never seen their creations in the design technology room. And now, she never will.

She doesn't react to this.

So I reopen the subject of Christmas.

There are no creeps, bores or alcoholics coming, no old enemies. There are practically no relatives, for God's sake. Peter's sister and her husband are great. And her older son is bringing the girl he's going to marry, a lovely new member of the family. Everyone's looking forward to it. Yet when I invited her, she reacted as if it were a trap.

'When I asked you for Christmas, it was a genuine invitation and not an attempt to control you,' I say.

'What do you mean?'

'You cited "family pressure" as the reason you weren't coming.'

'What? I don't remember that.'

Yes, you do.

I remind her of what we said in her kitchen only a week ago, when I repeated Peter's offer to fetch her and bring her back. She treats these occasions as something she has to escape from, but I have no idea why.

'When any of us invites you to something, we don't have an agenda. We just want to see you,' I say. 'The children want to see you.'

'Hm, yes.'

Maybe this is as far as we're going to get, this tentative acknowledgement that the family may not be a malign force. Maybe I have achieved something after all. I can ring my sister and say—

Suddenly she gets weepy again.

'It was so nice when your sister lived in the village and used to pop in for tea.'

This catches me right off guard.

'I can't say anything about that,' I say. She knows I have promised never to try and get her to leave her house and move to London. She also knows that none of us are going to move down there. So popping in for tea must remain a memory.

'It's nobody's fault,' she says reasonably, about the geography.

This is almost certainly as good as this call is ever going to get. I need to end it. Now. Maybe she feels the same, because she says suddenly, 'If I die in this operation, I do love you.' Then she adds, 'I'm going to go and have a good cry – when I can get the time.'

Maybe she's going to put it in her diary. *Do not say this*. I do not say it.

'I love you,' I say.

'I love you too.'

'I know,' I say.

'How do you know? How do you know I love you?'

This is possibly the strangest thing anyone's ever said to me, and also, in its way, brilliant. But brilliance is not what's needed here.

'Er! I don't know. Because it's logical that you would, I suppose.'

In other words, I'm going to have to take her word for it. She loves me, sure. But there are just so many things in the way. The treasure is real, but it's surrounded by countless obstacles and traps. And

I'm no Indiana Jones. Perhaps that's how it will end, with each of us on opposite sides of the jungle, knowing the gold is there, even seeking it, but never getting past the poisoned darts. And, in my case, dreaming of the dull life back in college with my adoring students, as quiet, unadventurous Dr Jones.

31 Visiting Ours

It is my last visit to my mother before she goes in to get her new hip. She has decided to have an epidural instead of a general anaesthetic and seems to be in good spirits.

'Epidurals are great,' I say. 'I've had two.'

'Oh,' she says. 'Good. I was a bit concerned that I'd hear the – you know – hammering, but apparently they give you something to make you drowsy as well.'

'Ah, a cocktail of drugs! Excellent. So you won't feel anything and you won't hear the sounds, like someone putting up an extension.'

'Ha ha, yes!'

She's sitting at the table, while I am bustling round the kitchen in that way she doesn't like. Except today it doesn't seem to bother her. No, I'm wrong. Something is bothering her. I can feel the tension, so I bustle even more. There's silence for a couple of minutes, then suddenly I hear a small voice: 'I'm frightened, that's all.'

And I realize it's her voice. And I think, *Shit, you're joking. Don't say that; anything but that. Please not that.*

She seems to be getting smaller right in front of me. A cold finger of panic crawls up my back and I say, 'Well! That's completely understandable. Who wouldn't be?'

Then I resume bustling. After a while, when the moment has passed, I go upstairs and put away my things.

When I come back down I remind her that we'll all be there on the day. Peter is going down the night before to take her in – she has asked him to – and I'm coming with the children on the train the day after. The children start school three days after the operation, so one of us at least will have to go back. Still, at the prospect of even a short, unsupervised stay at the house Peter's eyes have been lighting up.

'You'll be able to do tons of *tidying*,' he keeps saying, with an eagerness I've not seen since our courting days. And it's true: I am relishing the thought of filling bin bags with dried-up felt-tip pens and old sensible-shoe catalogues. I finish bustling and look at my watch.

'So! We'll see you on the fifth then!'

'Oh, but – well, I won't be here.'

'Well, no! You'll be in hospital. We're going to come and see you there.'

'Yes, but I'll be having this spinal block. I won't be – moving around.'

'I know. What did you think we were expecting you to do?'

She laughs.

'Handstands?'

'We're going to visit you in hospital. That's what people do.'

She thinks for a moment, as if searching for the correct response, and when she replies her voice is blankly polite.

'I see. That's very nice of you.'

'It's not "nice". It's what people do. We're your family!'

Did she actually expect us not to come and see her? She's as pleasantly surprised as if I were the woman from the post office. It occurs to me afterwards that, despite knowing she's not wired like most people, I haven't thought that I might need to explain *why* we're going to visit her. I'm making the mistake of assuming that she knows we'll want to be there, whereas she knows no such thing.

Back in the 1990s there was an American sitcom

called *Third Rock from the Sun*, about a crew of eccentric aliens who come to earth on a kind of field trip to study the humans. Their leader was played by John Lithgow and his 'cover' was a professorial post on the faculty of an American university. He was massively intelligent, but unlike Mr Spock and those ultra-rational types also quirkily imaginative, and only intermittently able to mimic human behaviour in a haphazard way that suggested creative tendencies mixed with a touch of Asperger's syndome. He and the crew were supposed to go back to their own planet, but he grew used to the strange, emotional humans. And the difficulties he encountered were as often with the members of his crew – who were having to pose as his family – as with the natives of planet Earth. He reminded me somewhat of my mother.

Peter says, 'She might really be an alien, of course.'

'What? Oh, ha ha.'

'Why not? It would explain one or two things.'

'Are you going to be doing anything useful this decade?'

'Apart from taking her to hospital and generally being the perfect offspring she never had?'

'If you were my brother I'd have pushed you off a cliff years ago.'

'Listen, mate, you want to be nice to me. If it wasn't for me, you'd be taking her in.'

He's right. Without him I'd be in a darkened room, shrieking.

The operation is a success. There's a small setback when she loses more blood than she's meant to and has to have a transfusion. And there's a bit of a problem when they run out of blood and have to get some sent over in a cab. Then there's a further teensy cock-up when the transfusing equipment fails and they have to inject it in by hand. Apart from that, it all goes swimmingly.

The four of us wait in the visitors' lounge, pacing. Well, I pace. Peter reads the paper and the children watch television. I've always thought people only paced in TV dramas, but I find myself walking agitatedly to and fro for two and a half hours, like an extra making too much of their part. When they finally let us in she is smiling and not looking at all as though she's just had surgery. She has already made friends with all the staff, and by the end of the first day has heard most of their life stories and secret dreams. She introduces us to them with her usual poise, as if we are all guests at a party, so that each bit of procedure, including having her catheter removed, becomes part of the social whirl. I am extremely proud of her.

The children give her the cards they've made, and when Peter takes them off for a play on the beach, I sit with a newspaper and read while she dozes. I like just being in the room with her. In these tranquil surroundings our stress levels fall dramatically. Each doctor, nurse and physio has a specific job to do that neither of us can micro-manage, which is wonderful. We have to shut up and stay in our places while they deploy their expertise. Both the order and the tranquillity have a magical effect. Unlike in our hospital in London, there are no police, no emaciated, twitching youths and no stringy-haired women in raincoats and slippers shouting. Finally, the hip package includes a sea view. It's as if we're on holiday, not just from the house but from ourselves.

In three days, though, the children are due to start school. I don't want to leave her, but I do want to settle them in. She doesn't want to come to our place, which I completely understand. Besides, her friend Debbie has offered not only to bring her home but to stay for at least two weeks.

'I think you'll find *she's* the perfect offspring, not you,' I tell Peter.

But Debbie works during the day and there is still no post-operative care plan. Eventually it emerges that social services are used to scrambling carers at short notice, indeed only arrange them once the operation has taken place. Mum's social worker, whom I meet later, is charming, and I'm amazed when the system does actually turn out to work. Mind you, I'm the only one worrying about it. My mother has refused to discuss it and has only recently agreed to recuperate in the new bed my sister has had delivered for the downstairs. She was going to sleep – she is five foot eight – on the two-seater sofa. I pointed out that with a new hip you're supposed to lie flat, but was dismissed as making her more anxious. At least with Debbie there we'll all be able to sleep more easily.

I love sitting in the sunlit room with her, just chatting and drifting. An operation is normally a huge stress-out, but we're having our most peaceful time for years. Then Peter collects me to get some lunch and the four of us come back for our last two hours with her. I'm already starting to miss her. Then a different nurse comes on, one I haven't seen, who will not leave us alone.

'Just doing the bed! Just popping in to change the drip! Just got to have you out now; the physio's coming. Just fiddling needlessly with the brochures,' and so on. When she runs out of things to lift up and put back again, she tries to engage each of us in conversation.

'Um, we don't have much time left,' I tell her. 'We're going back to London soon.'

She carries on regardless, eventually disappearing for a whole five minutes before returning with a broken computer console belonging to her nephew which she asks Lawrence to fix. By now even Peter is rolling his eyes. As for me, I'm feeling something far beyond annoyance. I realize with a jolt that I am gripped by a kind of terror, and it's exactly the same thing I felt when Lawrence was in the Special Care Unit as a baby, and one day a nurse made me wait an hour for no reason before she would let me pick him up. It feels terrible, worse than when we actually do have to go. Then that moment comes and I kiss her and go, crying only a little, to the car.

Will any of this make it any easier when she finally leaves us? Can you rehearse for death? Wouldn't it be great if you could get, like a death vaccination, a little bit of loss in the arm so the real thing doesn't finish you off.

On the way home I run over Cole Porter's words in my mind: 'Every time we say goodbye, I die a little . . .' When we get back I put out the children's uniforms for school, then go upstairs and look it up on Google. There's a link to YouTube. So many singers have performed it. Which one shall I choose? I start to type in Ella Fitzgerald, but no; my father took me to see her and I associate her with him. I need someone whose albums I don't have, someone different: Annie Lennox. Like my mother, she came from Scotland to London to pursue her ambitions. Like my mother, she is beautiful and impossible to categorize. She sings the song evenly, restrainedly, partly with her eyes closed, while an old home movie plays over her face. It's of two children playing, a boy and a girl. I gaze at it, half wanting to cry more. Then I go downstairs to find Lawrence and Lydia and kiss them, over and over again.

32 Cry If You Break Your Leg

Something weird has begun to happen to my reading habits. Instead of skipping to stories headlined *Fruit May Not Be Good for You* or *Three Hurt in Fondue Explosion** I'm finding my eye drawn to pieces about the ageing population time bomb. In the *Guardian*'s G2 section, instead of skipping to the snappy little pieces about Hollywood, I become fixated on a series of photographs of the dying. I read it, it makes me cry, then I read it again and put it in my bag. I can't seem to throw it away.

And it's not just the papers; the whole range of my sensory input seems to have been hijacked. In the car coming back from Mum's, instead of one of my old disco tapes I find myself listening to *Any Answers* and a call from a house-bound man who's paying for carers yet hasn't had a bath or a shave for two months. Two months! What a scandal. Even

* Both real news stories.

when I put the tapes back on I think about him, and Jonathan Dimbleby's aghast response. When I get home, I turn on *Saturday Review*, the evening arts programme, to discover a long item about how the writers of soaps deal with the unexpected deaths of their leading actors and decide how to write out their characters. Finally, I watch an entire ninety-minute documentary about Frinton.

I'm obsessed. I start collecting terrifying statistics and keeping them in my bag. I worry about Peter dying before me, or one of us becoming helpless, or both of us. My fears about my mother are now eclipsed by this new panic. If we in the developed nations go on the way we are, by the year 2030, three-quarters of us will be over ninety years old, and of those 110 per cent will be gaga. The strain on the NHS will be so great that millions of us will spend our declining years on hospital trolleys in corridors, on filthy mixed wards with our bits hanging out or left to starve with our lunches left on trays just beyond our reach.

'People are living too long,' says my friend Chris, who's about to be sixty. 'In the past, you and I would have been dead by now.'

Mike the knee surgeon agrees.

'You would have haemorrhaged to death in child-birth years ago,' he confirms breezily.

'It's terrifying; I wish I could have some control over it,' I tell my friend Richard.

'Rather than linger too long, I'd like to be able to choose a date in advance,' he says.

'But how would you know when it should be?'

I can't decide when to pre-order a cab to take me home from a party; how the hell would I know when I want to die?

Previously I managed to confine my worries to the potential emotional strain imposed by increased longevity on my marriage. Even allowing for our relatively late start, not to mention the two years between our first and second dates – Peter accidentally started another relationship – he and I could be looking at forty years together. And at an average of three tellings a year, that means I will have heard his personal turning point story about 50 times, his only-boy-in-rough-school-whose-father-had-a-car story 75 times and his reunion-with-oldest-friend-after-many-years story 120 times. With death in childbirth no longer an option, starving to death on a trolley may be my only way out.

But now I have a very real reason to read these

articles and watch these programmes. I have been managing, up to a point, to keep all this hypothetical. But I have a mother and she is about to turn eighty.

I decide to try and predict what may be expected of me by taking a step back to look at my family's track record. Let's see how many fevered brows have been mopped, how many bedpans emptied, how many wrinkly hands held.

My father had a strong sense of filial obligation. Even though he had dreadful scenes with his mother at various times in his life, he evidently did not let his feelings seep into his chequebook. He paid the rent on a very decent flat for her and his aunt, then when his mother died had Auntie to live with him. Then, when it when it became clear he was too impatient to put up with her full-time – I remember him yelling at her for blocking the lavatory by using too much paper, for example – he put her in a perfectly nice home. If any such homes can ever be said to be nice, this one was. I remember visiting her as a child, and there was definitely no wailing, no rows of chairs facing a blank wall and no scary smell. There was one small drawback, namely that the woman in the next bed believed they were in Dublin, and succeeded in convincing Auntie of it even though they were in north London. But that wasn't the fault of the home. In any case, Dad's place was not huge, and besides, by then he had acquired my stepmother, whose trays of etching acid did not combine well with Auntie's cups of digestive remedies.

The role of Dad's siblings was less straight-forward. The family correspondence boxes contain many letters with references to phone calls, recriminations and recitations of inadequacies, failures and slights. The underlying theme was who was suffering most or had gone to the most – unappreciated – effort. My father footed the bills but his brother and sister had the high ground when it came to time spent getting there, unreliability of transport, boxes of chocolates brought. Eventually to become the most successful one, at least in career terms, he was intermittently resented by the others, who endured long bus journeys carrying their chocolates and other, weightier burdens. But he had children, a blessing – or at least a distraction.

My mother's side was almost the complete opposite. While the Calmans stood by each other, complaining every step of the way, the McNeills pursued cheerfully detached lives. They simply did not appear to believe in family duty in the way my father's lot did. I can't speak for Mum's cousins, but in her immediate family there wasn't always the sense that they were even connected. Whereas the Calmans were like organs in the same body, the McNeills were discrete entities: people who had once shared a house but moved on. My grandmother and grandfather coexisted, their separate social lives focused on bridge and golf respectively, while their daughters got on with their marriages – or not, in my mother's case – 400 miles away. But that was the way they liked it. It seemed that for both generations expectations were about equal.

Granny and my mother exchanged entertaining letters full of shared jokes and gossip, a tradition my mother has continued to some extent, but the emotional webbing was absent. At least there was far less complaining. Among the Calmans, even the smallest personal crisis warranted urgent diary entries, phone calls and letters; to the McNeills, illnesses and even deaths merited no more than a line before moving on to the weather. McNeills didn't do moral support, as far as I can tell because it wasn't practical, a philosophy encapsulated by a particular remark of Granny's my mother frequently quotes. When faced with weepiness caused by any kind of emotional crisis on my mother's part, she'd apparently turn back to her housework, saying, 'Cry if you break your leg.'

My mother felt that this approach was somewhat less than nurturing, but then my grandmother had had so many real tragedies in her life, starting with the death of her own mother when she was thirteen, that to have had a mother at all would have seemed a luxury. To quibble about the *style* of mothering must have appeared to her petty-minded. And having survived a poverty-stricken childhood to marry and have a family, she lost her first child when he was four. My mother came next, and if it's true that people go one of two ways after the death of a child, more doting and over-protective or cold and distant, it seems that Granny went the latter. If she truly did fear that loving her next child might also end in the most unimaginable grief, it was hardly a conscious choice. Yet for my mother the death of her brother has had as much effect on us as any event in our own lifetimes. According to her, it explains just about all her maternal shortcomings, either real or as perceived by me.

As children we spent a week with her parents every summer, but as they got older and we became adults the trips gradually thinned out. The last one I specifically remember, when I was eighteen, was no less enjoyable than those of our childhood, but my grandmother had almost stopped going out. Her fear of being in an empty house, previously camouflaged by a busy social life, had grown into a phobia of being left alone even for a moment, and each morning she followed my mother from room to room, asking what our plans were for the day. To my mother's credit, she kept on answering patiently for the sixth and even seventh time, making lists of all our activities, potential and actual, which Granny of course ignored. My father, for all that he made free with his chequebook, would have replied twice at most before losing his temper.

My grandmother spent her final months in a hospital geriatric ward, but I persuaded myself it was entirely down to the distance and lack of funds. If she'd been nearer, if my mother had been richer, it would have been like the Calmans: lots of visits-plus-complaining like an indivisible boxed set. But it never would have been.

'She could do worse than end up by blowing herself up with the Ascot,' my mother said after one of her last visits before Granny was transferred. She didn't believe in clinging on for the slow, lingering end in an institutional, wipe-clean armchair. There was apparently no pressure on her to visit more often and even before she turned sixty she was already passing on the same philosophy to me: 'You don't owe me anything; you didn't ask to be born.' And I would think: *Phew, that's all right then.*

So, are we more Calman or McNeill? We seem to swing uneasily between the two modes. There is tea and listening, organizing and conversation, but without the intensity. That only comes with the arguing. Of course, my mother's detachment is rather liberating when you think that while fit and still relatively young my father might call at any time with a majorly debilitating setback, such as a cold.

'Could you bring me some orange juice? I'm marooned here,' he would croak down the phone, though he lived in Soho not Mull, and there was a supermarket underneath his flat.

My mother was far more independent. I've always been grateful for this self-containment, but it's left me with a less than solid idea of my obligations. With my father's family having been too emotionally involved and hers not enough, I'm not sure what the rules are.

What do I owe her? Shall I visit and clean the fridge / change the bulbs / file the bank statements / make casseroles, so I can say I'm doing something?

And at least when you've done those things they stay done; tête-à-têtes are unreliable, since our fragile equilibrium can always be undone by a single throwaway remark. So filing and making casseroles are safe. What's more, they mean some daughtering badges to put on my coat. If I fill the fridge and the ring binders – and signal my presence to the neighbours – maybe no one will notice the emotional gaps.

And then where do we go from here? How do we approach the last chapters of her life, providing help but keeping the independence which I know means more to her than anything? After all, I may not be able to stand her at times, but I do respect her rights. She has lived alone for many years and prefers it. I have told her that the worst I will ever inflict on her is more cleaning. I will never, never evict her. Even with a new hip she is not going to regain her previous fitness. She may even, unthinkable as it is now, one day lose her mental brilliance. These are all things that happen to millions. Yet there are no identikit solutions. She is a rare blip in the demographic graph, uncompromising in her autonomy, still pretty cool in her tastes and not clubbable. You would no more put her in a home than you would the Duchess of Devonshire. So we need to negotiate how to navigate these years with the maximum possible ratio of security to independence, and, ideally, the minimum of screaming. Unfortunately, negotiating is something neither of us is much good at.

My father avoided the fate worse than death by simply dropping dead at sixty-two. So it's looking as though I may well get to experience both types of ending: sudden and shocking, and slow and lingering. I can make notes and vote on which is worse.

And there all the time, also growing older, is my own family. They need me too. And they're the bit of my life that does work. In fact, I love them so much, and am so thankful for them, that I really would like to see as much of them as possible before my own time is up. Recently we had a wonderful week in the Canary Islands; everything – food, staff, facilities – was wonderful. But the hotel was at the end of a winding cliff road that absolutely terrified me. Every time the coach veered towards the edge I had to get Lawrence to distract me by naming his favourite cars beginning with all the letters from A to Z, and reciting bits of Eddie Izzard from YouTube. Then we got off the coach and the place was fantastic.

And that's how I feel about my life. It's not perfect. Peter and I argue and the kids argue and I shout at them all. But now that I've got here, I really don't want to leave the resort. I want to stay here, stop feeling guilty that I have the life my mother never had, and make the most of it. And I don't want to get back on the coach and look over all those drops. This may well make me the most appalling daughter ever born, but I can live with that. Or at least, at this stage, I can live with having had the thought.

33 Fallen Woman

It's six weeks since the operation. We arrive at the house to find a little box about the size of two cigarette packets stuck on the front wall.

'Did you see I got the Keysafe?' says my mother when we come in.

This is opened by a number code and has a spare set of keys in it so that if she activates the panic button the neighbours or emergency services can get in. This is the same panic button I tried to interest her in before. It was on a list of things I suggested getting before and after the operation, none of which she wanted to hear about. And while I could understand exactly why even talking about things like that made her feel as though she was being shoved prematurely into infirmity, I was genuinely concerned that with her newly bad hip she might fall over and no one would know, or that after the operation she might fall over and no one would know. And alongside that concern was a strong desire not to be phoned, sixty miles away, by a neighbour who'd seen her lying on the floor or heard her calling and couldn't get in. But, as with so many things, the actual issue became subsumed in a battle of wills.

On my various trawlings through the papers and Internet that seem to lead increasingly to stories of ageing parent disasters, I had followed a discussion by women with ageing parents which consisted almost entirely of sudden rushes to their houses when one of them had fallen over and the other couldn't lift them. My heart particularly went out to the woman who rushed down to her parents' home in Devon, which was a bit of a hassle as she had some years earlier emigrated to France.

But whenever I brought up the subject of panic buttons, carers or any other post-operative support measures, and especially when I pointed out how useful they were to this or that person I'd heard of, she said, 'You're making me anxious!'

I privately put this on a par with not making a will on the grounds that it makes you more likely to die prematurely, but there we were, the matter was closed.

Now that she has capitulated, I don't feel any sense of vindication and very little relief. Although I was irritated at the time by her refusal to consider any of these measures, I now feel slightly dismayed that she has caved in and accepted them. She has irrevocably moved further over into the realm of Oldness, where these and other accessories threaten to obscure her individuality. Why has she changed her mind?

'That's great,' I say. 'Good idea. When did you decide to get it?'

'My friend Gerald had a new hip at the same time as me and fell over at home.'

I know nothing about Gerald. He could be anything between a chap she bumps into now and then at the post office and a soulmate to whom she confides her innermost thoughts.

'Oh dear.'

'Yes, it really set me back.'

'Set *you* back?'

'Yes, I've been quite low about it.'

'But you've been doing fine.'

'Yes, but he had a fall, you see.'

'But you're *OK*.'

I cannot see why someone else falling over is such an issue. She knows people who have fallen over, had bits drop off them and in several cases died, without feeling it's automatically going to happen to her. Why should Gerald be any more significant –

unless she has embarked on a secret octogenarian romance and he fell on – or indeed off – her. But no, I think we would have heard by now. It would be: 'A man I am sleeping with in the village,' complete with precise description and address. Five minutes into this conversation I'm frustrated by her negative, non-life-affirming side rearing up again. Now of all times she surely needs to think positively, to be that breezy intellectual for whom corporeal matters are dull and trivial, the one for whom post-operative exercises are too tedious to bother with. Instead we're back to the part of her that all my life has focused on the downside. The part that worked for a pittance rather than ask for a rise, that stopped going to the theatre in case she fainted even though she never had, and stopped travelling even though she adored Europe and once upon a time had even lived there. This is the part that sees risk in the tiniest of ventures and comes up with ten reasons not to do something. We are going on holiday soon and, when we tell her, she worries that we may miss our flight because the airlines might not know that the clocks have gone forward.

It brings out the scoutmaster in me. I have my own anxieties about the wider world – mind you, these days that's rational – and feel that exposure to her life phobia may infect me. With my father gone there is no authority figure to counterbalance her fearfulness and so I react more strongly than in the past. I tell her she's 'doing fine', knowing that it is not even a terribly useful word, being an entirely subjective term whose meaning alters depending on who's using it. For instance, according to Peter she is fine because she 'can now go upstairs easily', whereas according to my mother herself the stairs are still a challenge, on which basis she is not doing fine at all. Constantly present in my mind is the knowledge that, whether she'd been given a new hip or a magic carpet, she never will be fine in any case because she cannot feel her feet. So even if she wanted to go somewhere it would be difficult. Nonetheless I want her to want to, so I shove this thought back and utter the word 'fine' with emphasis.

And while I know that any sensible daughter would be pleased that she's got the panic button, I can't bear it that she has chosen to identify with the one person she knows who's fallen rather than all the people who haven't.

Shortly after this, I am getting out of the shower one morning when I reach back to swish out the bath with the spray head and my knee locks. The last time this happened I was doing exactly the same thing, so I clearly haven't learned my lesson: don't clean out the bath. I am pondering this, and the fact that I really should get some breakfast, when I feel my head instantly draining, as suddenly and graphically as on one of those striptease pens which you tip to remove the lady's bikini. The next thing I know I am dreaming, then waking up with something smooth and very hard on my face. Christ, it's the *floor*.

'There was a sound like the chest of drawers falling over,' says Peter descriptively.

Lawrence, who was brushing his teeth at the time, is impressed.

'Your eyes sort of rolled up and you fell forwards,' he says. 'Like this.'

He does an impression of me rolling my eyes and falling forward, which definitely has potential.

'Do it again,' I say.

'I feel sorry for you, Mummy,' says Lydia. And she covers me with one of the extra large bath towels (John Lewis, Hotel range), putting a smaller one under my head.

Peter takes the children to school and I get up, slowly. My knee has unlocked in the fall but is pretty tender, there's a bump on my forehead and the whole left side of my face hurts when I touch it, but I can walk. By the afternoon, however, it's clear something is wrong. Peter is getting Lawrence from school and I am on my way downstairs to go out and get Lydia when the pain comes back and increases with each step. By the time I get to the last few I can only descend in a sitting position. I never make it to the door.

'Oh Mummy,' I want to say, 'help me, please!'

But I've missed my chance for all that.

Peter is meant to be dropping Lawrence, then going straight off elsewhere in the car, so I may not even see him. Lydia is waiting for me and I can't move. I can't ring the school because I can't reach the phone, and the only other person capable of movement is Lawrence, who will be here any minute, but how can I persuade the school to let him get Lydia? I am useless. The feeling of helplessness is horrible. I should have had my body frozen or something while it still worked. And while it still looked good. As I sit whimpering eight feet from the front door, without my phone, and unable to move my leg at all without causing myself excruciating pain, I take a moment to savour the memory of trying to persuade my mother to get a panic button.

'You could fall and end up lying there with no way of calling for help. And then what would you do?' were, I believe, my words at the time.

Gosh, how I am laughing now.

I am reminded of the woman in the ads for panic buttons which I first saw in the backs of the Sunday colour supplements at least twenty years ago. They ran with the caption '*Mrs Hope knows help is coming: would you?*' above a photograph of a grey-haired but rather over-rouged elderly female lying on her hall floor. Someone who was evidently equally fascinated wrote a piece about her in the *Observer*, wondering why Mrs Hope was always wearing so much make-up, and whether there was a Mr Hope, or if he had been disposed of to allow her to pursue a life of vice. Well, I can answer the one about the make-up. We fallen women have our dignity too, you know.

By evening the pain is no better, so I spend the night on a mattress in the sitting room. I can't get to the loo, so I pee into a stainless-steel mixing bowl which Peter puts on a chair with a towel underneath as a rather brilliant DIY commode. As I am peeing I think of his father, and the great Grimsdalian improvising gene. When the ferry he was on capsized on the Gambia river, all the passengers scrambled on to the upturned hull, but it was only Grimsdale who thought to prevent sunstroke by removing his underpants from under his shorts and putting them on his head.

'He would be so proud of you,' I say.

'I've never been able to get my pants off without removing my shorts, though,' he says.

I feel a bit badly for Peter. He's taken my mother into hospital, fixed the chair that goes up and down in her bath, fitted her raised loo seat, assembled her new bed, tuned her new TV set and done countless other jobs. Now he's meant to be having his reward, which is a visit from his friend Jason, all the way from Melbourne. Jason is here, but instead of driving round Scotland with him Peter's helping me pee into a bowl.

'I feel awful,' I say.

'Don't worry!' he says. 'One day you'll do the same for me.'

'Erm . . .'

The next morning, he wheels me into A&E. A gentle African man at reception takes my details and smiles, presumably pleased by the novelty of a patient whose ailment isn't drug-, alcohol- or husband-related. It is eight o'clock, and the only other people waiting are a woman with a bruised face and a man with no visible injuries being interviewed by three police officers.

'We thought we wouldn't come last night,' I tell the triage nurse. 'As you tend to be rather crowded.'

'It's always party time round here,' she says.

'I don't suppose twenty-four-hour drinking's done much for you.'

'Alcohol's our bread and butter,' she says, without so much as a smirk.

As Peter is parking the car when my name is called, one of the policemen offers to wheel me to X-ray, an undeniably bright moment in what is going to be a long, tiring day and a fairly tricky week. By a great piece of luck Mike the knee surgeon has his clinic that day. Someone offers to call him and he pops down to see me, looking much slimmer than usual.

'You've lost weight,' I say.

'Norovirus,' he says. 'I don't recommend it as a diet, though.'

I go home with crutches and instructions to put ice on it, take anti-inflammatories and rest. It's not broken but it looks like a snake that's swallowed a pig on David Attenborough, and cannot bear my weight. Mind you, nor can I. Lawrence and I invent our own version of Keysafe for when Peter's at work and our kind neighbour brings him back from school, leaving my key under the recycling box so he can get in without forcing me to hobble to the door. We call it 'Keybin'.

I decide not to ring my mother yet; it feels too like an attempt at one-upmanship. Besides, she might even worry about me. Peter is relishing the irony.

'You're the one who needs a panic button, not your mother!' he repeats, delighted with his brilliance. 'Hey, you could wear it round your neck. It could be connected to a shrink. Or maybe the deli: "Help, I'm panicking! Send chocolate!" And they burst in and adminster Lindt.'

'Yeah. Hilarious.'

'Or, when you panic about your mum—'

'Because *that's* really strange.'

'A toy panic button. A squishy ball not connected to anything, but every time you start panicking about her, you press this and it calms you down.'

'Ah, you're my squishy ball, darling. What do I need a panic button for when I've got you?'

'Yeah, well, I'm having the night off.'

A few days later I call her.

'I'm really sorry,' I say. 'I was going to come and see you, and now I can't.'

'Oh, I'm fine,' she says. 'Just take care of yourself.'

And she means it.

'I wanted to see you,' I say.

And I mean it too.

34 Unreadable

It's nine weeks since the operation. Feeling guilty because we haven't spoken for over a week, I phone. She's going to be eighty very soon and Claire and I have ordered her birthday present to arrive well in time.

'The new television's arrived,' she says. 'It's really lovely. I couldn't put it together though.'

'Well, no,' I say. 'Just leave it for us to do.'

By 'put it together' I assume she means plug it in, unless John Lewis have started trying to compete with Ikea and are now selling their audio-visual range in bits.

'It's all over the place. I'm afraid I couldn't help unpacking it because it looked so nice.'

'Well, just don't lose any of the cables or whatever.'

She has already done something to the new phone that makes it unable to take messages, and lost the booklet so I can't put it right. And it's not as though we're always inflicting confusing new technology on her; we first spent months trying to find batteries for the old one. At least she likes it; even with her tiny old telly the DVD player we gave her for Christmas has been a success. We have lent her the cream of our collection, films we know she will love too: *Shakespeare in Love*, *King Kong*, *The Matrix*, *Terminator 3*, and the seminal eco-thriller *Edge of Darkness*. She's seen parts of this three or four times, since we forgot to explain the scene selection facility or indeed the pause button, and so every time she had to leave the room, to go to the lavatory or get something to eat, she pressed stop and then started the whole thing again. Still, at least it is worth multiple viewings.

I explain that with the new set her aerial may need retuning for Freeview and we have a very normal conversation about how this might be achieved. I'm pleasantly surprised that the prospect of aerial retuning doesn't become a reason to reject the new TV. I've been trying to sell her Freeview for ages, on the grounds that BBC4 was invented for people like her. The first week I watched it, I saw films about Woody Allen, Lucian Freud and David Hockney, and a film about an ill-starred attempt to bring fame and glory to Andy Warhol's birthplace in

Slovakia, followed a few weeks later by a documentary about Robert Capa, the great Magnum photographer. It was as though the schedulers had her exactly in mind.

'You have to get this!' I kept saying.

'I really don't want to watch more television.'

'But this is *good* television. With no ads!'

You'd think from this she's the most highbrow viewer ever, but despite her great brain she's as susceptible to the lure of *The Bill* and *Bergerac* as anyone her age. This is just as well, as after half a day trying to tune it himself, Peter learns she's going to need a new aerial at a cost of £200. I don't tell her this, but we still can't get Film Four on ours, though Dave, the self-consciously 'laddish' comedy channel, works perfectly, as the children can attest.

Despite her apparently clear-cut status as AB1, however, she is able to slip across the demographic borders by constantly defying your assumptions. Her report of a lunch the day before at a local cultural association is not what I expect at all.

'It was so fucking middle-class,' she spits, sounding like someone you've just refused a quid to outside a pub.

'How do you mean? I'm middle class and I don't think it's a crime.'

I am being calm, probably because I'm not annoyed but genuinely curious.

'Oh, you know.'

'No. What? Boring, do you mean?'

'It was so – predictable.'

'What, all of it? Wasn't there a speaker or anything?'

'No! Just people wittering on about their holidays. So dull!'

'Oh. I've started being pretty ruthless about weeding out the dull stuff, but – maybe – I don't know. Do you want to? I mean, can you? I'd have thought you'd definitely want to just meet interesting people with—' I realize I'm about to say, 'the time you have left', so I change it to, 'with your being so interesting yourself'.

She's slightly defensive now.

'Of course, I do!'

'Well, good. I can never tell.'

I've just about avoided slipping into the quagmire of the ongoing issue of her social life. She complains of being bored and understimulated, and then, when I suggest doing something about it, such as going on a writing course – which she did a few years back and loved – she angrily denies there's a problem.

She had a couple of really lovely, very bright friends, but I don't know the rest. On the one hand, she believes that every individual has something interesting about them, yet at the same time suddenly bursts out with unfocused frustration and contempt.

Which is why I frequently revert to the relatively firm ground of her practical needs.

She has recently told us she can now manage the stairs and is ready to move back into her proper bedroom. This is great news, for several reasons. Apart from the obviously cheering prospect of her increased autonomy, we will no longer be greeted by the sight of her pants drying on the airer when we come in the door. Well, I assume we won't. She rebuffed my suggestion, on my last visit, that she put used underwear in the washing machine instead of soaking it in the downstairs sink and hanging it all over the sitting room, like John Osborne meets Chinese New Year. And the idea of giving it to the carers was right out.

'I'm taking control of my life,' she'd retorted, apparently to appeal to my interest in her independence, yet managing to overturn in a single phrase the efforts of the entire feminist movement to free women from the domestic yoke.

'Anyhow,' I'd pointed out, 'you've got about four thousand pairs. You'll probably never have to wash any again.'

'So about the bed. Peter can sort it out when we come next weekend.'

'What d'you mean?'

'Take it apart and so on, and move it upstairs. It's ideal, because we'll all be there at once.'

We're all going to assemble for her birthday. So there'll be four pairs of reasonably strong hands to do the job.

'Oh no, that won't be possible.'

'Why not?'

'I'm still waiting for the raised loo seat.'

And there you have it, the quintessential Catch-22 of being elderly in Britain: she is trying fulfill the Department of Health's brief to live independently, but she can't reinhabit her bedroom because the upstairs lavatory is too low.

'Well, when's it coming?' I say. 'I said you'd need two ages ago.'

'I don't know.'

'Well, there must be some kind of time frame. Have you rung them?'

'It's not that simple. There are so many depart-ments.'

'Never mind that. Ask the nice social workers. It's their job to help you.'

'No, actually it comes from another department.'

'That doesn't matter. They're supposed to coordinate these things. Every day they deal with people who've got horrendous problems. A call from you will be a treat.'

I know this reluctance to ask for things isn't unique to her; it's bizarrely prevalent across that whole generation. But it's so incongruous. With this level of passivity, how on earth did they win the war?

'It's in hand, thank you.'

This is her code for 'Now piss off', which I combat with an 'OK!' followed by a swift email to the social workers before I go to bed. I can see, stretching out before me, ten or fifteen years of trying not to take over, taking over, being beaten back, retreating, advancing, troubleshooting bits of it, though not always satisfactorily, and wanting to rip my own head off and hers. How much responsibility am I meant to take here? How much do we owe not just our parents but anyone? It should be obvious, yet it's clouded by people's expectations and the huge discrepancies between them. A Good Daughter helps but never tries to control, foots the bill but doesn't impose her values. Christ, it sounds like the charter of the UN; we've got no chance.

The conversation is winding down – at least I think it is. Then suddenly she revs it back up again.

'Who got me that book, *Dissolution*?'

'I did, why?'

Peter and I have both read the Tudor thrillers by C. J. Sansom and are huge fans.

'There's something quite extraordinary about it, something no one's mentioned.'

'What's that?'

'I know three people who've read it and not one of them has mentioned it.'

It takes place on Romney Marsh, not very far from where she lives. The monastery it's set in is presumably fictionalized, but I wonder if—

'The typography is *abysmal*.'

There is a pause.

Eventually she says, 'It's unreadable!'

Another pause. I am genuinely stumped.

'You know, a lot of people say they can't read Dickens or whoever because it's too difficult, when it's just because they use the wrong font, the margins are too narrow and there isn't enough spacing between lines.'

'Is it too squashed together?'

'The individual words are too far apart!'

'I don't have the hardback,' I reply feebly. 'But you could get it from the library. It might be different.'

But I know this is not what she wants.

'I think I'd better go and get on with the supper,' I say.

'What?'

'We're clearly heading into one of those pits and I just can't see the point.'

'You're not interested! I thought you'd be interested.'

'What can I say? I got you this as a present and all you do is complain about the spacing.'

'What? You're so touchy!'

'OK. Well, I'll see you next weekend.'

'Next weekend?'

'Your birthday.'

'Oh. All right then.'

Maybe because I'm not so much angry for a change as defeated, she sounds startled, like someone pushing against an open door.

'Call me if you need anything.'

'Oh. Yes. All right. See you then.'

'Bye.'

I take out a bottle of wine. Peter says, 'You've already got one open. How is she?'

'I really don't know,' I say. 'I have no bloody idea.'

35 The Second Synagogue

I've often thought that even if I weren't half Jewish,
if I was going to have a religion it would be Judaism,
as it has the most smiting. Another aspect I strongly
relate to, though this is cultural and as far as I know
not in the Bible, is the generous amount of time
given over to complaints. For example, when a guest
is late – I do this myself – there's a tendency to dwell
on the various mistakes they've made to bring the
crisis about. This is me – with guest:

Guest: 'Sorry I'm late. There was terrible traffic
on the A205.'

'You took the A205? Why did you take the A205?'

'Er, I dunno. I thought—'

'That's the worst way! Never go that way. Next
time . . .'

I then launch into a detailed description of the
entire route from their place to ours, banging on like
a demented taxi inspector, while Peter says periodically, 'So you're here now. That's great,'

As we now live south of the river, and a good few of our friends live north, this can take quite a while.

This focusing on the less, shall we say, positive aspects of an issue is enshrined in a number of Jewish jokes, of which the most famous – and easiest to remember – is probably the Tie Joke.

A man is given two ties by his mother for his birthday, a blue one and a red one. He unwraps the present, puts on the red one and goes down to show her.

'So,' she says. 'What's wrong with the blue one?'

Many people make the mistake of thinking this is purely a Mother joke. But it isn't. I know, because of the Desert Island joke. I like the Desert Island joke because it makes such a true observation about religion's factionalism and its emphasis on bolstering identity by emphasizing what we are *not*, but also because it expresses this – not purely Jewish but a bit Jewish – thing of emphasizing the negative. But recently it took on an even greater value for me when I read a book called *Family Heaven, Family Hell*, which explores the reasons why family gatherings such as Christmas dinners are so stressful and suggests various ways to handle them. Since the person

I get most stressed over is my mother, who doesn't come to family gatherings, I quickly decided the book couldn't help me. But then I read something which lit up for me like a bulb. The author describes how we often like to cling to our negative experiences, almost wallow in the 'bad things' our families do to us. She likens it to keeping them in a kind of emotional safe deposit box, and taking them out and looking at them, to keep proving over and over again how hard done by we are. Fuck, I thought. That sounds exactly like me. I was so embarrassed I decided for the moment to keep that realization to myself. The last thing I wanted was Peter saying, 'Oh God, yes, that is *so* you. You do that all the time,' and so on. I wouldn't be able to stand it. So, instead, here is the Desert Island joke.

A Jew is stranded on a desert island. After about twenty years a ship sails by and rescues him. The captain comes ashore and says, 'You haven't done too badly for yourself here. You've made shelter, a food store, a garden ... And what are those two buildings you've put up?'

And the man says, 'That one is the synagogue I go to.'

'Oh,' says the captain. 'And what's the other one?'

'That's the synagogue I *don't* go to.'

What can I say? As this book ends my task is just beginning. I've got to start taking down that damn second synagogue.

Postscript: A Lid on It

Now that Lawrence and Lydia are both having tea in the mornings we have started using our big pot, normally saved for guests. It is deep blue and of that classic, satisfying round shape. Also, using real tea – a habit of Peter's I found peculiar when I first met him – has proved easier, as well as far more tasty, than four tea bags.

One morning I come down to find Peter holding the broken pieces of the lid.

'Don't worry,' he says. 'I can mend it with superglue.'

But we don't have any, and we keep forgetting to buy some, and the pieces of the lid remain on the windowsill, clustered together hopefully like refugees waiting for their passage to a better life. And to my intense annoyance, he continues using the teapot *without the lid*.

'You can't,' I say. 'This is just like my mother!'

'No, it isn't.'

'It is! You're using it with no lid!'

'Your mother puts a saucer on it.'

'And you think by not doing that it's somehow different. *And* it gets cold way more quickly.'

'The children don't like it hot.'

'God . . . !'

'Look, I'm going to fix it. Just shut up, OK?'

We go about our business, he to his work and me to my knee exercises. Then at four the children come back from school and both want tea, and so do I. And as I open the cupboard to get the mugs I see this smart little steel saucer that came with an old espresso cup we no longer use. And I think, ooh, that will sit on the teapot just nicely. And then I realize what's happening and a shudder goes through me.

Suddenly opposing forces are clashing inside me. I don't know if I can resist the saucer – it might destroy me. I must resist the saucer! But also I want my tea.

This is the vortex, where decades of struggle come to a head. My whole identity is at stake. My head is throbbing. I must have my tea. But I cannot use the saucer! No! Please . . . ! My hand trembles. I reach for the saucer . . .

The saucer triumphs. I pour the tea and fix it in my gaze.

'Don't get too comfortable,' I tell it. 'The lid will be glued: it will, it will!'

Acknowledgements

My thanks go to my editor George Morley, who gave me mojitos and almond cake, Mark Lucas, the greatest agent ever, and my husband, Peter Grimsdale, who listened endlessly to my doubts and read all the rewrites. This book could not have been written without them.

My grateful thanks go also to the 'other mothers' in my life who have at various times been there for me: Rose Kendall, Pat Huntley, the late Midge Stumpfl, Karen Usborne, Beryl Vosburgh, the late Jill Tweedie and Patricia O'Shea. Also those whose inspiring example I am trying, however ineptly, to follow: Angela Holdsworth, Vida Adamoli, Sarah Litvinoff, Patrick Tatham and Teresa Howard. I am also indebted to Lawrence and Lydia Calman-Grimsdale, two amazing people who make me laugh every day.

I'd also like to thank my embarrassingly numerous psychotherapists and counsellors of the past, especially Juliet Hopkins, Dr F. Gainza, Caro Bailey, and Polly MacDonald at the Alchemy Alliance.

And on the home/work front Sophie Doyle, PA and Multitasking Queen; not all tranquillizers come in jars. Also my sister Claire, for her encyclopaedic memory of everything from the exact colour of the Goblin Teasmade to *Invasion of the Bodysnatchers*, the novel. Her notes should be published in their own right.

Finally I'd like to credit the books that helped me with this one. *Remind Me Who I Am Again* (Granta) by Linda Grant is a tragic and funny book about the mother–daughter relationship, ambivalence and impending loss. *Family Heaven, Family Hell* (Fusion Press) by Jo-Ann Grzyb is an excellent and practical approach to surviving Christmas and all those other flashpoints for family trouble. *When You & Your Mother Can't Be Friends* (Bantam Doubleday Dell) by Victoria Secunda is compassionate, honest and as good a self-help manual as you're ever likely to find. *The Dance of Anger* (Thorsons) by Harriet G. Lerner provides great insight into this much misunderstood emotion. Claire Tomalin's *Samuel Pepys: The Unequalled Self* (Penguin) has raised the bar for nonfiction and Mr Pepys has also boldly led where I have feebly endeavoured to follow. And Michael

Ondaatje's *Running in the Family* (Picador) is a masterly portrait of an eccentric family in an exotic setting, beautifully written, funny, outrageous and, like all truly great books, capable of making you feel just that bit better about life.